I0540208

## Praise for *LifeSkills*

*"I love this book!* **LifeSkills** *touches upon many of the most critical topics in life … such as integrity, change, communication, and conflict resolution … but it does so in a way that begged me to keep on reading. The author is disarmingly honest as he shares his deep Christian faith, his outstanding business success, his own life experiences, and all the things he has learned to make your work and relationships so much better. This book is a jewel! Read it and read it again. You'll be better off if you do."*

—DR. ALAN ZIMMERMAN,
HALL OF FAME SPEAKER, COACH, AND AUTHOR

*"***LifeSkills,** *by Larry Dobbs, is no ordinary book. It is filled with inspiration, life accounts, failures, and successes. It offers infinite wisdom based on a lifetime of learning through personal experiences and missional purpose.* **LifeSkills** *will surprise you, inspire you, encourage you, and offer you nuggets of wisdom that will prove beneficial to you and your future. This book will not let you go until you have read every page. Enjoy, be inspired, and learn!"*

—PASTOR M. WAYNE BLACKBURN,
LEAD PASTOR AT VICTORY CHURCH,
LAKELAND, FLORIDA

*"I heartily recommend Larry Dobbs' new book. He speaks powerfully and practically to show that doing life and doing business are not mutually exclusive. Anyone in any field of endeavor will be enriched by this fine book."*

—MARK RUTLAND, PH.D.,
AND PAST PRESIDENT OF ORAL ROBERTS
UNIVERSITY AND SOUTHEASTERN UNIVERSITY

*"I approached Larry's book LifeSkills with great curiosity, as Dobbs Publishing and my father's businesses National Parts Depot (NPD) both sprang out of the then-emerging classic Mustang craze around the same time, both in Florida, and were inter-meshed and inter-related in many ways. In fact, I believe my Dad purchased most of Larry's inventory when Larry decided to shift 100% towards publishing. Reading this book, as much as they shared in common, there was equally as much that they did not, in terms of background. But regardless of those differences, they both shared one critical virtue… Integrity. And from that common core and foundation, success flourished. Taking risks, fighting through adversity, surrounding themselves with quality people, and being savvy enough and researched enough to win more than they lost… They both shared every single characteristic, all of it flowing from pure integrity. My read through Lifeskills left me realizing that two different men, from different backgrounds and upbringings, could achieve tremendous things by following common and timeless virtues, all of which are beautifully laid out and explained by Larry. Bravo!"*

—RICK SCHMIDT,
VICE PRESIDENT AND CHIEF OPERATING
OFFICER, NATIONAL PARTS DEPOT

*"From Larry's humble beginnings, as son of a sharecropper in Georgia, to the owner and publisher of several magazines, to total reliance on a loving God throughout his life, **LifeSkills** is more than a biography, a devotional, or a management book. It's all of the above. And it's excellent reading. I read the book in two sittings and appreciate Larry's use of the Scriptures to bring it all together."*

—JIM CAMPBELL,
PRESIDENT AND CEO OF THE RADIO TRAINING
NETWORK OF 47 CHRISTIAN RADIO STATIONS

*"Larry Dobbs was a faithful friend and loyal member of ABBA's House church during his time in Chattanooga. His abilities were many and certainly encouraged the work of our church. I am glad he has written **Lifeskills**, and that so many will benefit from its clear message."*

—DR. RON PHILLIPS,
PASTOR EMERITUS, ABBA'S HOUSE, CHATTANOOGA

*"Mr. Dobbs has a gift for distilling life's most important lessons into practical, actionable insights. Whether in relationships or leadership, his guidance comes from experience, empathy, and a deep desire to help others grow. This book is a meaningful extension of the impact he's had through LifeSkills—and a must-read for anyone seeking more purpose and connection in their journey."*

—MIKE YAGER,
CHIEF CHEERLEADER, MID AMERICA MOTORWORKS

"**LifeSkills** *gives a quick look at one of the bravest men I know. Larry Dobbs knew what it looked like when things went well and when they went bad, but was never afraid to try! He would always gather all the facts he could to make a decision. I remember one particular time that Larry started three magazines at the same time. After a few months of losing money ... and it was a lot of money, Larry called the leadership team to his office. He told us that he would make a decision by the end of the day ... right or wrong, he would make a decision. Larry didn't have a problem making decisions. That decision was to "shelve" two of the magazines and sell the third. This didn't stop Larry from starting more magazines. I think he might have waited at least a day or two before we started another very successful automotive magazine. He would often share these LifeSkill Nuggets with his leadership team, and this book is filled with* **LifeSkills** *that he lived daily in his work and his life. Don't be surprised if you are so encouraged that you want to start a new magazine! It had that effect on me!"*

—CURT PATTERSON,
PUBLISHER OF *THE LAKELANDER MAGAZINE*

*"Little did I know how much my life would change when Larry Dobbs called in 1979 to offer me the editor's job for his young magazine, Mustang Monthly. Not only did it launch my dream career as an automotive journalist, but I also spent 18 wonderful years working for Larry, a born entrepreneur whose deep Christian faith, humor, and adventurous business spirit resonated throughout Dobbs Publishing Group. Everyone employed there was blessed to have Larry as a mentor, not only as a boss but also as an example of how to succeed personally. I'm glad to see that, through this book, he is sharing with the rest of the world his knowledge and passion for helping others navigate through the journey of life."*

—DONALD FARR,
EDITORIAL DIRECTOR OF THE PATE MEDIA GROUP

"Some skills are appropriate for a job or single tasks. However, the most valuable skills are those usable for all tasks, all the time. In this book, Larry Dobbs has provided guidance for developing and using a broad range of skills for life. Everyone who reads this manuscript will be better equipped to succeed in life. Read and succeed!"

—REVEREND DR. TERRY RABURN,
SUPERINTENDENT, PENINSULAR FLORIDA
DISTRICT ASSEMBLIES OF GOD

# LIFESKILLS

# LIFESKILLS

Discovering Relationship and Leadership Skills

# LARRY G. DOBBS

LifeSkills

Copyright @ 2025 by Larry G. Dobbs.

Printed in the United States of America. All Rights Reserved. No part of this book may be reproduced in any form or by any electronic or mechanical means, including information storage and retrieval systems, without permission in writing from the publisher, except by a reviewer, who may quote brief passages in a review. Published by Larry G. Dobbs.

ISBN-13: 979-8-218-69474-6

Edited by Joni M. Fisher

Original Cover Design and Formatting by Damonza.com

# TABLE OF CONTENTS

Introduction. . . . . . . . . . . . . . . . . . . . . . . . . . . . . . . .xiii
**PART 1** . . . . . . . . . . . . . . . . . . . . . . . . . . . . . . . . . . 1
1: Create Your Future. . . . . . . . . . . . . . . . . . . . . . . . . . 3
2: Build Courage and Determination . . . . . . . . . . . . . . 9
3: Discover Your Uniqueness . . . . . . . . . . . . . . . . . . . 21
4: Find Your Passion. . . . . . . . . . . . . . . . . . . . . . . . . 27
5: Take Risks . . . . . . . . . . . . . . . . . . . . . . . . . . . . . . 37
6: Live by Integrity. . . . . . . . . . . . . . . . . . . . . . . . . . 45
7: Develop Your Influence . . . . . . . . . . . . . . . . . . . . 51
8: Communicate Effectively . . . . . . . . . . . . . . . . . . . 61
9: Resolve Conflict. . . . . . . . . . . . . . . . . . . . . . . . . . 69
10: Adapt to Change . . . . . . . . . . . . . . . . . . . . . . . . 75
11: Create Your Life Plan . . . . . . . . . . . . . . . . . . . . . 81
12: Stay Relevant . . . . . . . . . . . . . . . . . . . . . . . . . . 85
13: Prepare for Obstacles . . . . . . . . . . . . . . . . . . . . . 89
14: Overcome Setbacks . . . . . . . . . . . . . . . . . . . . . . 95
15: Encourage Others. . . . . . . . . . . . . . . . . . . . . . . 109
**PART 2** . . . . . . . . . . . . . . . . . . . . . . . . . . . . . . . .**113**
Nuggets of Wisdom . . . . . . . . . . . . . . . . . . . . . . . . 115
Afterword: Reinvent Your Life . . . . . . . . . . . . . . . . . 145
Acknowledgments . . . . . . . . . . . . . . . . . . . . . . . . . 147
About the Author. . . . . . . . . . . . . . . . . . . . . . . . . . 149

# INTRODUCTION

This book is for those who want to improve their relationships and leadership skills and become exemplary work, home, and community influencers.

The principles outlined, including many of my stories, contain guidelines that led me to become a successful businessman and a recognized relationship and leadership trainer. These skills inspired me to discover personal fulfillment, motivated me to become a person of faith, and proved that Christianity and success do work. All quoted scriptures are identified by the translation used.

Applying these fundamentals, you'll accomplish goals in your personal life, plus you'll be able to develop the skills necessary for enjoying healthy and happy relationships. Also, you'll learn leadership skills needed to become an effective leader.

This book is not focused on theories; instead, it's proven principles, guidelines, and methods I used to create a multimillion-dollar publishing business.

Let's begin by telling you how my life began.

## Humble Beginnings

When I was a teenager, my mother told me about my birth.

"It was a freezing night in January when I gave birth to you, Larry. Your daddy and I were sharecroppers, some said tenant farmers. We never owned a home but moved to a different landlord's old wooden shack every year for your daddy to farm their land."

As my mother shared the story of where they lived at my birth, I was reminded of all the old houses we had always lived in. Old houses in such disrepair, we could often see chickens running beneath the old house's floorboards. We 'young'uns' hoped the next house we'd move into would be better. It never was. Our lives were like those of many of today's migrant farm workers.

Mother said, "Every year when the crops were gathered, daddy's share would barely be enough to pay the debts we'd charged taking care of our family that year. He knew he'd been cheated out of his hard work of plowing, planting, and harvesting the crops our family had worked so hard to care for and cultivate. Each year, when the crops were gathered, we knew we'd be moving again.

"On that night, your daddy made a warm pallet for me to lay on in front of the fireplace while he went to get the midwife. We were poor, and poor women used midwives to help them birth their babies because we couldn't afford hospitals. The midwife daddy went after had helped me give birth to many of my babies before. But I was uneasy as Charlie drove his rickety old truck away on them slick, muddy roads. Your daddy told your brother, Ed, who was only thirteen years old, to keep the fire in the fireplace burning until he got back. It was already getting dark when Daddy left."

Then, Mother said, "Son, I was so afraid, and I prayed hard that your daddy would make it safely back. Since a strong winter storm had started pouring rain and sleet on the tin roof of the weathered old wood-frame house we lived in.

"But, when my labor pains got really bad, your brother, Ed, got so scared; he'd never seen a woman in pain giving birth, especially not his mother. Before long, panic got the best of him, and he ran out through the woods in the storm toward the Brinson's house. They were our closest neighbor, who lived more than a mile away. He was crying and hollering for help. By now, it was 9:30 at night. I had birthed many babies before you, so I knew you'd be born pretty soon. But your daddy hadn't made it back. So, I was all alone when I gave birth to you. After you were born, I was all by myself for what seemed like hours, waiting for Daddy and the midwife to get back. All I could do was pray to our Lord that you'd be a healthy baby."

Mother said it was midnight when Daddy finally got back with the midwife. His old truck had gone into the ditch, and it took him a while to get it back on the road.

She said, "As soon as they got back, the midwife cleaned me and you up, and, seen to it we were both okay. Then, she placed you so you could begin nursing. Son, I was so thankful!

"Two weeks later, your daddy took us to Moultrie to see Doctor Conger. He did a complete examination of both of us. He said he was astonished that we were both very healthy. And, I said, 'Yessir, I know, 'cause God answered my prayers.' Then, he said he couldn't believe I'd given birth to a healthy eight-pound baby boy all alone on a freezing January night! Then, he said, 'Mrs. Dobbs, this baby's survival and good health is truly a miracle! God must have something special for this little fellow's life.'"

As Mother finished telling me this, she gave me a loving hug and said she believed Doctor Conger when he said God had something special planned for my life.

That doesn't mean my life has been a cakewalk. Instead, it's been filled with many challenges to discover that 'Something-Special' that the doctor promised my mother.

I shared my humble beginning, so you'd know my life began with a miracle.

I was the seventh child of hard-working, devoted parents. They did their best to raise seven children, scrimping together to provide for our family. I remember what my mother often told me, "Larry, God has a bright future ahead for you, son. All you have to do is trust in Him with all your heart and never give up!" I later learned this is a paraphrase of God's promise in the book of Proverbs in the Holy Bible.

My life's story shows that success doesn't depend on where or how you start. It depends on where you're heading and the future you're creating.

I have a memento in my office, a tangible reminder of my sweet mother. It's an old ceramic butter churn that Mother used to churn milk into butter five nights a week. She'd then sell milk, butter, and eggs on Saturday afternoons to regular customers who awaited her arrival at their homes each week. She used the money she earned to supplement the $10 Daddy gave her weekly for groceries and school clothes for us children. A difficult life, but they never gave up.

If I could start my life over, I'd finish my formal education and become a lifelong learner much sooner. However, no one can start over. Thus, I encourage you to start creating the future you desire to become the person God intended. I enjoy fast cars, and I've learned you can't make progress looking in your rear-view mirror. So, beginning today, I encourage you to focus on the future so that your life will be filled with thankfulness, not regrets.

# PART 1

# 1

# CREATE YOUR FUTURE

*"You can't go back and change the beginning, but you certainly can start where you are today and change the ending."*

–C.S. LEWIS

WISDOM DID NOT come early in my life. When I was sixteen, I foolishly dropped out of school. Why? Because I was failing English.

Ironically, failing English made my career choice years later to become the founder, publisher, and CEO of a multimillion-dollar magazine publishing company sound unbelievable. Additionally, I was awarded an honorary doctorate in Literary Letters due to my success as an international publisher. Yes, God has a sense of humor. He will provide a miracle if we refuse to give up and if we repent from our foolish ways and turn our lives over to Him.

Now, back to my foolish decision to quit school when I was sixteen, I went to work for my oldest brother at his

Pure Oil Service Station in Moultrie, Georgia, pumping gas and changing tires. It was a low-paying job and back-breaking work. Yet, I believe it was at that time that God created my love for cars. Some say I've got motor oil in my blood.

I worked there for a few years. One day at lunch-time, my good friend Max, who worked down the street at Gaines Supermarket, and I decided to walk uptown to the Moultrie Pool Hall for lunch.

Max and I often played pool during our daily lunch hour. I was winning the game that day, which was unusual, when Max said, "Larry, we should get outta this one-horse town. Let's join the Air Force."

I said, "Sounds like a good idea, Max. Let's do it."

The pool hall was directly across the street from the Federal building, where all the military recruiters' offices were located. We finished our game and washed down two chili-cheese dogs with SunDrop Colas. Next, we walked across the street to enlist in the U.S. Air Force.

However, when we got upstairs, a sign on the recruit-er's office read, 'Out to Lunch.' We turned to leave when a big fellow wearing a navy-blue uniform with lots of stripes and a white Dixie-Cup hat (U.S. Navy's standard uniform) opened his office door and asked, "Who are you boys looking for?"

We told him we had come to join the Air Force, but the Air Force recruiter was out to lunch.

He grinned and said, "Fellas, he's always out to lunch. But you boys are in the right place. Walk over here to my office." Then, he said, "You know the Navy has an awe-some air force. It's U.S. Naval Aviation."

Max and I were convinced to enlist on the spot.

Next, I called my mother to tell her I'd joined the Navy. Later that afternoon, Max and I were on a Trailways bus, heading to Atlanta to be inducted into the U.S. Navy.

The recruiter had told us that he'd stipulate we were joining together on the 'Buddy Plan.' When we got off that bus in Atlanta, it was the last time I saw Max for several years. So much for the Navy's 'Buddy Plan.'

After one year, the Navy offered me six months' pay to re-enlist for six more years. I served another six years until my enlistment expired, being honorably discharged as an E-5.

I re-enlisted mainly because the re-enlistment bonus was enough for a down payment on a used 1965 Mustang. Was this an epiphany? Perhaps. Years later, I published a special interest magazine for Ford Mustangs.

During those seven years in the Navy, I matured in some ways, but still didn't have my personal life together. Regretfully, during that time, my marriage fell apart. The failure was primarily my fault due to my unbridled arrogance. Thankfully, there were no children. Though still immature and impetuous, I thought I'd learned a lesson. However, God was at work. His plan and my sweet mother's prayers would one day come to fruition, as God was still methodically teaching me valuable life lessons.

You've probably heard it said: "If you continue doing what you've always done, you'll continue getting what you've always gotten." However, I have an addendum to that axiom: "But not for long; soon, you'll begin getting less and less."

So, I enrolled in the local junior college, applied for and received my high school diploma through the GED program. Years later, after becoming a successful publisher, I received an honorary doctorate.

I also began improving my vocabulary beyond the undesirable words I'd learned in the Navy. I read self-help books, including *30 Days to A More Powerful Vocabulary*, Dale Carnegie's *How to Win Friends and Influence People*, *Discovering the Laws of Life* by John Templeton, *The Power of Positive Thinking* by Norman Vincent Peale, *Think and Grow Rich* by Napoleon Hill, and many others.

The most important thing I learned was that success requires a commitment to learning, regardless of your career or vocation. Knowledge sets you apart, helping you stand out instead of fitting in. The books you read, the places you go, and the interesting people you meet influence the future you hope to attain. Understand that personal growth is a continual process.

Use whatever resources you can obtain, including formal education, research, and AI (Artificial Intelligence), to continually grow and learn. Set goals. Seek to achieve the unique purpose that God created you to accomplish. Don't allow failures to stop you from becoming the person God created you to be.

*"When the person you could have been meets the person you are now becoming, will there be a cause for celebration or heartbreak?"*

—SETH GODIN, AUTHOR AND INTERNATIONAL MARKETING EXPERT

# R E V I E W

- Behavioral psychologists say there are four sources of happiness in life:

  1. A future to believe in and look forward to.
  2. Having someone to love who loves you.
  3. Doing work or activities you enjoy that you believe matters.
  4. Having good health and enjoying what you are doing.

- To succeed in life, you must stand out, not fit in.

- Scientific research shows that people who stand out are typically lifelong learners, attend church regularly, live longer, have a better quality of life, and enjoy happier, fulfilling relationships. So, be a lifelong learner who's a stand-out.

- The best way to have the future you desire is to create it. However, human nature craves comfort and predictability, seeking to recreate the past versus the determination required to create a better future. Know that contentment and complacency are not the same. You can have both progress and contentment.

- Practice improving your strengths, unique skills, and abilities. It's far more productive than trying to improve your weaknesses.

- The world and culture change faster and faster. Being flexible, regardless of your age, is essential to remain relevant.

- If you're in the second half of life, this can be exciting or the deadliest season. As we age, the natural progression of human nature is to change from being productive to being comfortable and less active. Next, we become complacent, which brings firmness of mind. Before long, like cement, the brain becomes set in place, impossible to stir.

- Choose now to become the person you were created to be. For thirty days, make personal growth and learning your daily priority. Develop these lifestyle habits. You'll be excited to see the difference this will make in your life.

# 2

# BUILD COURAGE AND DETERMINATION

*"Courage faces fear and thereby masters it. Cowardice represses fear and is thereby mastered by it."*

—DR. MARTIN LUTHER KING JR.

FOR ME, COURAGE and foolish choices began at an early age.

It was a cool September morning, and I looked forward to fourth grade. Our family lived about a mile from the paved road, where my sister Cornelia and I caught the school bus to Culbertson Elementary School. She was going into the sixth grade. Halfway down the dirt road, Cornelia started laughing.

"What's so funny?" I asked.

She continued laughing and said, "Larry, you're not gonna like your teacher. She's really mean!"

It was at that moment that courage kicked in. It was my first memory of exercising courage. I suddenly turned around and walked in the opposite direction.

Cornelia hollered at me, "Larry, where are you going? You're gonna miss the bus!"

Hollering back, I said, "I ain't going to a school where there's a mean fourth-grade teacher!" I was nine years old.

That's when I remembered my two good friends went to Reedy Creek Elementary School, on the opposite side of the county. I thought, shucks, I'll just catch the bus with them and go to Reedy Creek Elementary School in the fourth grade! So, I caught the school bus to Reedy Creek Elementary with Carlton and Jerry. The fourth-grade teacher at Reedy Creek told me to go to the school office. Armed with nothing more than the enthusiasm of a nine-year-old, I registered myself in school. Yep, it was simpler times back then.

I knew it would be a while before my parents learned I had changed elementary schools because, as poor share-croppers, Daddy and Mother never attended school functions, PTA meetings, or parent-teacher meetings. Therefore, they had no idea where I was attending school. As the seventh child, I got away with much more stuff than my older siblings.

Months later, Mother and Daddy discovered I was going to Reedy Creek, not Culbertson. It happened one day when Cornelia got mad and told on me. Mother was quite upset!

However, Daddy just shrugged and said, "*Igannis* Sarah, don't fret about it. At least the boy's going to school." *Igannis* was Daddy's favorite slang word, which meant 'by golly.'

When you want something bad enough, you muster the courage to do whatever is needed and make the tough decision to change things. This takes courage. Living with fear and trepidation is not scriptural, and it's not for me. After coming to faith, God's Word assures me that I'm a new creation in Him.

Courageously, I made a tough business decision years later when courage was tremendously needed. It was a Friday afternoon in early October. My company was a relatively new startup. Our finances were quite strained, surviving month-to-month. I only had one magazine at that time. That magazine had only a thousand paid subscribers and two dozen paid advertisers. I had nine employees, and we were really pinching pennies.

That day, I learned a valuable lesson about courage.

My secretary came into my office about closing time and said, "Larry, there's a fellow in the lobby who says he'd like to talk with you."

I asked her what this guy was selling to be working so late on a Friday afternoon.

She said, "I'm not sure, but he says he's from *Hot Rod Magazine*."

At the time, *Hot Rod Magazine* had over a million subscribers and nearly two million readers, including newsstand buyers. Therefore, I told her to invite him into my office. He introduced himself as Terry Shiver, a regional sales representative for *Hot Rod.*

Years later, Terry Shiver was promoted to publisher of *Motor Trend Magazine.*

He said that *Hot Rod Magazine* was going to publish a Mustangs-only special issue in January. Then, he said the magazine's back cover was available if I'd like to buy it to advertise for my *Mustang Monthly Magazine.*

The dictionary defines courage as the state of mind that enables one to face hardship or disaster with confidence and resolution. Acts 14:22 advises us to be courageous because we must go through many hardships in this life to enter the kingdom of God. Nevertheless, courage usually isn't easy.

There was no way I could afford to buy the back cover of *Hot Rod Magazine.*

However, Terry got me thinking when he said, "Larry, this issue is going to only be about Ford Mustangs, and the advertiser—who always buys the back cover of Hot Rod— doesn't sell anything for Mustangs, so he's opted out of the back cover of the January issue."

At the time, Hot Rod's parent company, Petersen Publishing, didn't have a magazine devoted to Mustangs. Later, they would.

He asked again, "Would you like to buy the back cover of this special January issue?"

Nearly two million people will be reading *Hot Rod's* special Mustang issue. All these folks will be able to sub-scribe to *Mustang Monthly Magazine.* Mine was the only monthly magazine about many of those readers' favor-ite cars, Ford Mustangs. I quietly prayed, asking God for wisdom and guidance.

I felt a peace in my spirit about buying the back cover of *Hot Rod's* January issue, even though I didn't know how much it would cost. I said, "Yes, I want to buy the back cover of *Hot Rod Magazine's* January issue!"

He handed me the contract to sign.

The full-color back cover of *Hot Rod Magazine* was going to cost $20,000.00! My hand quivered. I was dumbfounded at the price of that one-time advertise-ment, which equates to approximately $80,000.00 in today's dollars!

I seriously considered changing my mind. I had every reason to be apprehensive. Banks wouldn't loan me money. They didn't understand the accounting dynamics of a publishing business's deferred subscription income. My financial balance sheet showed a negative net worth of nearly $100,000 due to deferred subscriptions that had yet to be fulfilled.

At the time, I had a thousand loyal *Mustang Monthly* subscribers who were renewing for $10 per year at a 90% rate, equating to a *bona fide* projected income for the coming year of $90,000. Plus, the additional new subscriber and advertising income represented a projected income of nearly $200,000 for the coming year.

I continued praying in the weeks ahead, awaiting the release of *Hot Rod's* (Mustangs only) special January issue. This was a big, big decision.

I was nervous for the next three months and prayed for a miracle. Toward late November, *Hot Rod Magazine's* January issue was scheduled to go out to a million subscribers and be displayed on tens of thousands of national magazine newsstands. it was delayed. I was totally stressed out!

I called the Petersen salesman to ask why the magazine wasn't on sale yet.

He said there was a glitch at the printing company. The magazine distribution would be a month late.

I planned to give my employees one week's pay as a Christmas bonus on Thanksgiving weekend. However, I didn't have enough money in the bank to pay the bonus; I barely had enough to pay them for their current work week. Therefore, I called everyone in, apologized, and told them not to come to work the following week because we had a shortage of cash reserves. However, God was at work in my life and theirs. Unbelievably, all my employees showed up for work the following Monday, not expecting to get paid. These folks were a wonderful group of devoted people.

In mid-December, I still did not see *Hot Rod Magazine* on the newsstands. I called Petersen Publishing's advertising salesman again, asking when the January issue would be on area newsstands.

He said, hopefully, it would go on sale around Christmas time.

Christmas was on Thursday, so on the first Monday after Christmas, I anxiously went to the post office, hoping there would be lots of paid subscriptions in my mailbox with checks enclosed. This was before the proliferation of credit cards. At the post office, I slowly opened my mailbox. Inside were two envelopes: an invoice for $20,000.00 from Petersen Publishing, Hot Rod's parent company, and my monthly utility bill. Feeling quite dejected, I hung my head to leave.

## Courage Supplants Caution: When God Knows It's Your Best Option

That's when our jovial postal carrier, Otis, hollered across the counter, "Larry, what are you driving today?"

"I'm driving my van, Otis. Why?"

He laughed and said, "Well, that's good because I've got eight large bags of mail back here for you!"

Eight bags of mail in one day! My employees spent the entire day opening mail with checks enclosed. God had rewarded my faith.

Later, I discovered an important fact about direct marketing, a fact that direct marketers have always known. The biggest day of the year for incoming direct mail response is the **Monday after Christmas**! That's why your mailbox will be filled with dozens of catalogs around Christmas. They know it's the time of year when you're in a buying mood.

Was it a coincidence? Or did God orchestrate the glitch with *Hot Rod Magazine's* printer so that the January issue, with my full-page ad, would be delayed a month, until the Thursday just before Christmas? A coincidence? Perhaps, but I believe God used it to show me His miracle-working power! I don't believe in coincidence.

I've learned that God's timing is always the right time. I knew I had been following the prompting of the Holy Spirit to purchase that expensive $20,000 advertisement. Thus, in His timing, God had miraculously shown up.

On that one day, over $80,000.00 in paid subscriptions arrived in those mailbags! It is equivalent to over a quarter of a million dollars today. Checks kept coming for weeks.

Seeing all those envelopes, some with the words, *'Check Enclosed'* written on them, caused me to remember, many years before, when selling copiers for Lanier Business Products, Jim, my district manager, would often say, "Dobbs, don't ever forget, the two most beautiful words in any language are, Check Enclosed." For me, they were beautiful words that day! My employees were also thankful and blessed. They received two weeks' bonus pay in their January pay envelopes!

Soon, other magazines began competing with *Mustang*

*Monthly Magazine*. However, we remained number one until I sold Dobbs Publishing Group years later.

See chapter 14, 'Prepare for Obstacles,' for more of my business story.

## Courage and Determination Began at an Early Age for Jay

Jay was only sixteen years old, working at a Ford dealership cleaning vehicles until 6:00 PM every day after school. The boy put in 12-hour workdays during the summer.

Part of his job was removing all the vehicle's hubcaps every night so they wouldn't be stolen. One day, carrying an armful of hubcaps, he bumped into the dealership's new general manager and dropped all the hubcaps.

The boy was fired on the spot. He repeatedly asked for his job back with no success. So, the boy wrote to Henry Ford II. He explained what happened, writing that his family was a loyal Ford family, and when he was old enough, he would buy a Mustang. He closed the letter asking Mr. Ford if he could help him get his job back.

Soon thereafter, the dealership called the boy and said, "I don't know who you know in Detroit, but if you want your job back, you've got it."

Later in college, the same boy wanted to work at a Rolls-Royce dealership, but the owner said there were no openings. However, the boy started washing cars at the dealership anyway. When the owner noticed the young man, he asked what he was doing. The young man replied that he would work there until he was hired. He was immediately hired. That young man with courage and determination was Jay Leno.

## Courage to Accomplish Your Goals Will Often Require Creativity

I served in the U.S. Navy as an aircrewman on a Boeing Super Constellation Early Warning aircraft. These were huge 3-tail aircraft like the ones flown by TWA airlines in the 1960s and 1970s. I was shocked to learn that my Navy job was discontinued due to the advent of over-the-horizon radar. Equally shocking, I received orders to report for duty as an air crewmember aboard a small twin-engine reconnaissance airplane jettisoned off aircraft carriers' decks. Too often, the small airplanes never got airborne. Oh no! Not me! I didn't re-enlist for six years for this!

I went to my base commander, a full Navy Captain, and expressed my chagrin. He laughed, uttered a few expletives, and told me he didn't care and to get my butt ready to report to duty aboard an aircraft carrier. Leaving his office, I thought, Lord, I need your help!

When I returned to my barracks, I told my friend about my dilemma. He said he knew about a Navy job rating I'd probably like; 'Training Devices." He said the supervising director over the T.D. rating for the entire Navy was an enlisted man, a 30-year E-9 (Master Chief Petty Officer). His office was in Washington, D.C.

I decided to go to Washington, D.C., to visit with this fellow. So, I caught a round-trip MAPS flight on a Navy plane to D.C. for the weekend. Sailors could fly on these flights at no charge if seats were available.

Thankfully, I was able to make an appointment with that Master Chief. I told him how I had re-enlisted for six years to serve in a rating that had been discontinued. I was to be assigned to a rating I didn't choose. The Chief seemed very understanding. He told me to take the MAPS flight back to Newfoundland and expect a different set of orders to be there.

A few days later, when my new orders arrived, the Base Commander called me in. Using his worst sailor's language, he said he had no idea who I knew in Washington D.C., but to get my a** out of his office.

*Ha Ha!* I gladly got out of his office.

That courageous trip to Washington, D.C. helped me get assigned to attend the U.S. Navy's Training Devices school in Memphis, TN!

The following week, I reported to T.D. school in Memphis, Tennessee. After I graduated from training, I served as a Flight Simulator Instructor in Virginia Beach, Jacksonville, and Key West, Florida. This became possible only because I had to find courage and show creativity, which led to bold acts.

As you pursue success, always remember you are your best advocate, especially when life becomes challenging.

# REVIEW

- Being courageous is standing up for what you believe, even if you're the only one standing. That's when God's anointing will help you stand up and stand out.
- When God's at work, there's no doubt who's at work because that's when miracles happen! I've courageously proven this in my lifetime, and so can you!
- Courage is not the absence of fear; but having the faith and determination to face those fears, continuing toward your goals and objectives in life.
- Your courage reflects how much you believe in yourself and your dreams.
- Have courage when you're giving a presentation. Allow yourself to pause for a few seconds. Yes, it's uncomfortable, but it exhibits incredible courage, showing that you're the person in the room who's in control.
- Have the courage to exhibit diligence and determination to show you're unwilling to quit.

*"Faith is having the courage to continually see it in your mind and hold it in your heart. Then, you'll ultimately see it with your eyes and hold it in your hands."*

—Larry G. Dobbs

# 3

# DISCOVER YOUR UNIQUENESS

*"God's gifts and his calling can never be withdrawn."*

(Romans 11:29 New Living Translation)

*"In his grace, God has given us different gifts for doing certain things well. So if God has given you the ability to prophesy, speak out with as much faith as God has given you. If your gift is serving others, serve them well. If you are a teacher, teach well. If your gift is to encourage others, be encouraging. If it is giving, give generously. If God has given you leadership ability, take the responsibility seriously. And if you have a gift of showing kindness to others, do it gladly."*

(Romans 12:6 New Living Translation)

WE'RE ALL SIMILAR, yet each of us is unique. A few things that make us similar are the desire for personal freedom, self-esteem, and discovering our life's purpose. However, each of us has unique, individual goals.

This book reveals why it's essential to discover your individual uniqueness—the things that set you apart.

## This Boy Traveled a Difficult Road to Discover His Uniqueness

Young Jesse's family lived in a two-bedroom house, where Jesse slept on a cot in the kitchen. Anytime his brothers or dad walked by, they'd kick the cot, waking him up. He felt like a loser growing up. As a young man, Jesse got a job on the night shift, plucking chicken feathers in a local chicken processing plant. Jesse's job was for individuals who weren't capable of much else.

As a young boy, Jesse was smaller than his brothers and fourteen years younger than his next-oldest brother. Sadly, his dad told him he was a mistake. His two older brothers were mean alcoholics. They'd often beat him up and tell him he was a 'retard' and that he would never amount to anything.

In school, he was the target of every bully on the playground.

Jesse dreamed of becoming a ventriloquist. He often practiced with sock puppets. Then, one day, Jesse made a new friend named Dave. Dave helped Jesse feel better about himself. Yet, Dave wasn't a person. He was Jesse's ventriloquist's dummy. Jesse continued passionately pursuing ventriloquism.

When he got old enough, Jesse left his dysfunctional family and joined the military. The time was World War II, and because of his ventriloquism talents, Jesse was assigned duty as an entertainer for the troops. He became part of a military comedy group called The Stars & Gripes. Jesse enjoyed making people laugh so hard they'd be in tears. For the first time in his life, he felt good about himself.

Once Jesse left the military, he finished college and moved to New York City to pursue an acting career. However, he continued to struggle with feelings of inferiority, remembering his brothers' harsh words, "You're a retard. You'll never amount to anything."

Things didn't improve for Jesse for the next seven years.

However, Jesse's uniqueness and his dream of acting miraculously changed when he caught the eye of Andy Griffith, an actor starring in the Broadway play, "No Time for Sergeants." Andy, at the time, was also putting together the cast for his new TV series, "The Andy Griffith Show," about the simple life of folks living in Mayberry, a small North Carolina town.

In his unique nervous tone, Jesse asked Andy Griffith if he thought he'd be a candidate for this new show.

Andy thought it over, deciding that Jesse could play the part of a nervous and jerky deputy, providing a humorous spin on the show.

Soon after the show began, Jesse Donald Knotts became Mayberry's nervous deputy. His humorous character was a perfect fit because of his uniqueness. Soon, Don Knotts, as Barney Fife, became loved by millions.

*"Find ways to embrace things that make you unique, and you'll unlock the ways you can make a difference in the world."*

—DAN MILLER,
AUTHOR AND CREATOR OF *48 DAYS TO THE WORK AND LIFE YOU LOVE*

Passion is directly related to your uniqueness. It's key to unlocking your life's possibilities.

# R E V I E W

- Write down what your values and beliefs are. Not your parents' values and beliefs, not your spouse's, not your boss's, not your teacher's. Yours. Keep this list for future reference.
- Focus on the work you enjoy and your best skills.
- Your values and beliefs set you apart from others. They are key to what makes you unique.
- Next, identify and list your God-given gifts. Ask a trusted friend to offer their input and views. Creating this list will prove beneficial in discovering your uniqueness.
- Combine your unique gifts and skills with your life experiences. Focus on work you truly enjoy and your skills.
- Refuse to listen to the naysayers. Instead, listen to your inner voice of gladness. That's how the Holy Spirit will speak to you, reminding you how God has uniquely wired you. He created your individual uniqueness.
- Note: If continuing education is needed, create a plan now for getting it.
- God created you to be His vessel, whose purpose is to spread the fragrance and knowledge of Jesus Christ everywhere your life takes you.

*"Who you are is the person God designed you to be. Thus, it's vital that you know who you are. An acorn doesn't become a pine tree. It must become an oak tree and will grow into exactly what God intended it to become."*

— JOHN J. SCHERER, THE SCHERER LEADERSHIP CENTER

# 4

# FIND YOUR PASSION

## Age Doesn't Dictate Passion

MICHAEL WAS ONE of my finest employees, a sharp nineteen-year-old who worked as the shipping and receiving supervisor for DPG's (Dobbs Publishing Group) MotorGear Collectables Division. Michael had recently married Vicki, another fine DPG employee and a beautiful young lady, who worked as one of our magazine's production and creative coordinators.

Early one afternoon, Cheryl, my Administrative Assistant, came into my office and said, "Larry, Michael would like to talk with you."

My employees knew I had an open-door policy, so they could talk with me whenever they needed to. So, I told her to please ask him to come right in.

Michael said, "Mr. Dobbs, I've always heard you say it's important to follow one's passion if a person wants to be happy in life."

Selfishly, I thought, I'm fixing to lose Michael. Trying

to sound agreeable, I said, "Yes, that's true, Michael. What's on your mind?"

He said, "I think you know that my brother, Ronnie, and I sing gospel music. And now, we're planning to begin singing gospel music for a living. Mr. Dobbs, It's our passion."

To which I said, "Well, Michael, maybe y'all should test the waters and do a few local gigs, to see if you can make a living singing gospel music."

Michael immediately retorted, "No, sir, we're getting a bus and going on the road touring as The Booth Brothers, singing gospel music. Mr. Dobbs, you know my dad was a member of The Rebels' quartet?"

I said, "I do. But, Michael, what does Vicki think about this?"

To my chagrin, he said, "Mr. Dobbs, she said that I should pursue my passion and that she would gladly go with me and be supportive of my career choices, whatever they were."

Right then, I knew I was about to lose two wonderful employees! Therefore, trying to be supportive and spiritual, I asked Michael if I could pray with him. I prayed that he and his brother Ronnie's lives and future as a gospel singing group would be blessed and directed by the Lord.

Fast forward ten years. After selling my publishing company, I began living summers on Signal Mountain, Tennessee, near Chattanooga, and winters in Florida. That's when one Sunday morning, Dr. Ron Phillips Sr., the lead Pastor of Abba's House Church, also known as the Central Baptist Church, asked me aside to talk while we were having coffee before church. He invited me to preach that Sunday night's message for the Abba's House congregation. Abba's House was the largest church in Chattanooga, Tennessee. Nervously, I agreed, and then I prayed fervently all afternoon for God's anointing. I needed the Holy Spirit's guidance, especially about the topic of my message. I only had a few hours to prepare. I felt impressed to speak on the power, purpose, and positive results of having passion.

While I was praying, I remembered what young Michael Booth had said that afternoon years ago when he told me he was leaving DPG to follow his passion of singing gospel music. I wondered how Michael and Ronnie Booth's gospel group was doing, so I went online to see what groups were currently popular in Southern Gospel Music.

To my amazement, I discovered Michael and Ronnie Booth and The Booth brothers were voted the number one Gospel Singing group in America just the Saturday night before! Wow! That news made my Sunday night message powerfully anointed!

## How Do You Know If You Have Passion?

*"You have passion when you want something bad enough to fight for it, to give up your time, sleep, and comfort for it...It's all you dream about. Life seems useless and worthless without it... You'll gladly sweat for it and fret for it and abandon all fear of the opposition for it...you're willing to simply go after it with all your capacity, strength, and sagacity, pursuing it with faith, hope, and stern tenacity. Neither cold, poverty, famine, sickness...nor pain of body and brain can keep you away from the thing. So, dogged and grim beseech and beset it. Because God has filled your heart with passion for it!"*

—Berton Braley,
"If You Want a Thing Bad Enough"

Are you passionate? Do you welcome each new day with hopeful anticipation, or do you dread getting out of bed and going to work in the mornings, feeling tired and grumpy at the end of the workday?

*Forbes* magazine reported that every day, over one million people in the United States call in sick. Research further revealed that most of these people were neither sick nor passionate about their jobs and careers.

Thus, I suggest that if you're not enthusiastic about your work, it's probably time for a career or job change. However, I don't recommend that you suddenly abandon your primary source of income. Instead, try blocking out time for purposefully transitioning to get involved in the work and activities you genuinely enjoy and in which you'll feel engaged. Create a timeline and a plan to move to a career you'll enjoy.

Passion is far more likely to find you when you use your unique gift and Godly calling. Doing work you love feeds your soul and fulfills your career life. Plus, when you have passion, you're more likely to be your authentic self, fully realizing your competencies and achieving your life's possibilities.

A November 2024 Gallup poll survey revealed that 51% of the United States workforce is unsatisfied with their work and is looking for an opportunity to change to another job or career. What's alarming is that only 19% say they are satisfied with their work.

Which group are you in? Those in the 51% who are unsatisfied have not discovered their passion and are not pleased with their job.

Whenever interviewing new employees for my publishing company, we looked for the three important traits: integrity, passion, and savvy, in that order. Integrity is the most important since passion without integrity will quickly get things off track.

These were the same traits I looked for when planning to launch my company's fifth automotive magazine, a magazine about Chrysler performance cars entitled *Mopar Muscle*. My editorial director suggested we interview Greg, one of our contributing writers, for the magazine.

When Greg came to Florida for the interview and saw all the passionate automotive enthusiasts working in our offices, he was like a kid in a candy store. We were quite impressed with his integrity and passion. Therefore, we hired and trained him for the skills he'd need to be the editor of *Mopar Muscle Magazine*. That magazine was an instant winner. Greg was a great hire for Dobbs Publishing Group.

At Dobbs Publishing Group, passion for the job was an important trait we looked for when hiring our key team members.

> *"That each of them may eat and drink, and find satisfaction in all their toil—this is the gift of God."*
>
> (ECCLESIASTES 3:13 NEW INTERNATIONAL VERSION)

Ecclesiastes was written by King Solomon, the wisest and richest king in Biblical history.

## Questions to Ask to Determine Whether You Have Passion:

- Do you enjoy the daily work you're doing?
- Are you pleased about where this career is taking you?
- Are you satisfied with who you're becoming?
- If not, are you developing a plan for transitioning into something satisfying?
- Write out a list. What are your unique interests, gifts, and strengths?

## Facts to Know About the Power of Passion:

- Passion will embolden you while paralyzing the opposition.
- Passion overcomes fear, becoming the fuel of miracles.

- Passion generates enthusiasm, energy, and creativity.
- Passion is contagious; so contagious that others will catch it from you.
- Doing what's possible doesn't require passion, but without it, the impossible will remain impossible.

## It's Important to Put Borders Around Your Passion

- Passion must be submitted to obligations. Be sure to prioritize your current commitments and responsibilities before you decide to pursue your passion.
- Caution: Integrity comes first. Never allow your passion to compromise your integrity.
- Passion must be bathed in prayer and led by the Holy Spirit.
- Make sure your passion stays focused through research and planning. Passion without purpose and prayer will likely end in a train wreck.
- Seek wise counsel to ensure your passion is guided with wisdom.

# R E V I E W

Age doesn't determine passion. These people all became successful in their pursuits:

- Elizabeth became Queen of England as a teenager.
- Tommy Hilfiger opened his first clothing store at nineteen.
- Future shipping magnate Cornelius Vanderbilt, at seventeen years old, borrowed money to start his first endeavor, a ferryboat. Vanderbilt later became one of the wealthiest people in the world as a shipping magnate and head of a national railroad empire.
- Bill Gates founded Microsoft, becoming a multibillionaire.
- Debbie Fields was barely twenty years old when people began bragging about her chocolate chip cookies. So, she began baking and selling her cookies. She failed several times to rent a kiosk in a local mall. Even her parents and potential investors laughed at her. Later, in the 1990s, she sold Mrs. Fields Cookies for one hundred million dollars!

As senior citizens, they all followed their passion:

- Helping to make barefoot waterskiing famous, Banana George Blair was still so passionate about the sport at the age of 93 that he skied barefoot on Lake Eloise for the amazed crowd of onlookers at Cypress Gardens, Florida. George Blair was a man who lived his life with passion. At age 91, he parachuted onto Lake Eloise, thrilling the hundreds gathered there.

- Colonel Harlen Sanders, at age 65, depressed after receiving his first Social Security check, became passionate about selling his grandmother's fried chicken recipe. He then launched Kentucky Fried Chicken. Now known as KFC.
- Passion is not an addiction. Addictions feed the flesh's appetite. Passion fuels your spirit, energizing you to strive for excellence and fulfillment.

*"God doesn't want you to live your life in random chaos like a 'pinball', hoping not to get bounced around too hard before being shot out again the next day, only to be bounced around some more. Your destiny is not to finally slide by those swinging paddles into oblivion."*

—DAN REILAND, JOHN C. MAXWELL'S RIGHT-HAND MAN WHEN JOHN PASTORED IN SAN DIEGO

*"Too many workers regard themselves as wage slaves, and too many workplaces appear to be places of pain, not passion, populated by individuals who are underutilized and undervalued. Often, their great ideas die with them."*

—WARREN BENNIS, CHAIRMAN OF THE LEADERSHIP INSTITUTE

# 5

# TAKE RISKS

*"Studies prove the reason people quit growing is because they're unwilling to take risks."*

—M. Wayne Blackburn, Lead Pastor,
Victory Church, Lakeland, Florida

The first few years after Judy and I were married, I continued to bounce from job to job, never afraid to take risks. My view was that I was looking for a job when I got this one. I was still immature, impatient, and uncertain about the direction of my life.

Yes, Judy and I were happily married. However, we soon decided that perhaps I wasn't doing what I was best suited to do. I asked myself some tough life and career questions to determine if I was on the right track.

Neither Judy nor I liked my answers to those questions. (See the passion questions on the preceding pages: Questions to Determine Whether You Have Passion.)

Interestingly, the following Sunday, our church's

pastor said something life-changing in his message, "I believe God is redirecting some of our young folks' lives and careers today. Perhaps it's time for you to step out, take a risk, trusting God to redirect your life."

Driving home, I told Judy, "I think he was talking directly to me."

However, Judy wasn't sure that making a quick career change was in our best interest. She had recently resigned as a psychiatric social worker at the county hospital, making good money, to become a stay-at-home mom with our new baby son. However, I had decided that it was time for me to change career directions.

Be aware that when you decide to change your career or life's direction, the loudest voices you'll hear are doubters and skeptics, like Debbie Field's parents when she had a passion for beginning Mrs. Field's Cookies. Few people will be at the train station when you're heading out to chase your dream. This is also a big reason why quitters stop growing. They listen to naysayers and become afraid to step out in faith and take a risk.

Not me. The following Monday morning, being the impetuous person I am, I went to the local bank for a $5,000 loan to start a magazine about Ford Mustangs. The loan officer conducted a credit check and made phone calls to verify my income and current employment status. He learned that I was employed by the local newspaper, which was owned by *The New York Times*. He also learned that I was their highest-paid salesman.

Then, he asked me, "Larry, why are you quitting an excellent job making great money to start a magazine about horses?"

I replied, "Mustangs are cars built by Ford Motor Company, not horses."

The banker laughed out loud, looked across his desk, and said, "Larry, you're crazy!"

After selling my successful publishing company for millions of dollars, I reflected on what that banker said years earlier. I'm not sure what happened to him. Recently, I recalled his scathing words as I read leadership blogger Brandon Burchard's quote:

*"If no one thinks you're crazy, you're probably not yet operating at the outer limits of your potential."*

—Brandon Burchard, Author
and Leadership Trainer

What about you? Are you operating at the outer limits of your potential or just hanging out in your life's comfort zone? Perhaps it's time for you to act.

*"How long can you afford to put off who you really want to be? Separate yourself from the mob. This is your life. You aren't a child anymore. Decide to be extraordinary and do what you were created to do…now!"*

—Roman Philosopher Epictetus

Getting back to my story about trying to get a loan. That banker finally agreed to loan me $5,000, but only as a second mortgage on our modest Sun-State home.

Meanwhile, when I signed for the loan, Judy was at

home taking care of Jason, our two-month-old baby. She had no idea I had just taken out a second mortgage on our home. I do not recommend this strategy; my passion and ambitious actions were foolish.

Judy was distraught and disappointed that I hadn't talked with her before taking out a second mortgage against our home. Yet, she tried to be understanding and supportive. She was always my #1 encourager throughout our 30-year marriage.

## God Gives Second Chances with Forgiveness and Restoration

Sadly, years later, Judy passed away from a malignant brain tumor. The next several years were difficult, as I remarried quickly and went through a divorce.

But, thankfully, after a few years, my son, Josh, suggested I ask Melody, a beautiful lady who attended my LifeSkills class, out for dinner. Melody had been divorced for several years. She later told me that she hadn't dated since getting divorced. She had no intention of dating or ever getting remarried again. However, she said she admired and greatly respected me, having been in my LifeSkills class for many years. So, we began dating, and after a few months, I asked her to marry me.

Thankfully, Melody said, "Yes."

We were married months later. And, for the past several years, Melody has brought joy, happiness, and fulfillment back into my life.

I have taken many risks. Some did not pay off well.

Although I was semi-present at my core business during these times, thankfully, my competent and focused leadership team ensured that Dobbs Publishing Group remained profitable. A few examples:

a. In the eighties, when folks were decorating their homes with country and early American themes, I decided to open a 'Country Store' in a nearby shopping center. Two years and $300,000 later, I closed it.

b. Being a collector of antique toys, I purchased *Toy Collector Magazine*. Yes, it was a magazine, but it had no relation to the car magazines we published. I sold it back to the original owner a year later. This risk cost me $200,000.

c. Flea markets have always intrigued me. On Monday, as I toured the Webster, Florida, flea market, I saw an abandoned old warehouse for sale on the outskirts of town. I went inside for a look-see. I thought, "Shucks, I could turn this into an antique mall." So, I bought it and built cubicles to rent to potential vendors. I named it Memory Lane. It's still there. Some say it's still a big success. However, in the two years I owned it, I lost $180,000.

d. I've taken a few bad risks, including this one. I decided to launch a magazine of Americana called *Down Memory Lane*. I'm not sure how much money we lost before shutting it down, but it was substantial. The Dobbs Publishing Group employees nicknamed it 'Down Money Drain.'

All those bad risks are nothing compared to the good decisions and profitable risks I've taken in business. My life is evidence that not all risks will be profitable. Thankfully, I've taken far more profitable risks than unprofitable ones.

# R E V I E W

Considerations before taking a business risk:

- Do you enjoy the career and work you are doing? If you are unsure, draft a Ben Franklin balance sheet listing on opposite sides of a page 'likes' and 'dislikes' of your current job and career. This will help you make a tough decision.
- What are the specific possibilities of your current career, and where will your life's current direction take you? Are you pleased with that destination?
- Reflecting on your career and lifestyle, are you satisfied with the person you're becoming?
- Next, list your proven work and life skills, identifying your strengths and weaknesses. This detailed list will enable you to become fully aware of who you are and what possibilities and future opportunities you might have.
- NOTE: Always seek to improve your strengths, but don't waste too much time trying to improve your weaknesses. In the future, seek to use your strengths, and if possible, delegate your weaknesses.
- Successful people are willing to make tough decisions and mistakes. Make the decision!
- Caution: Avoiding risks will ensure you'll have a life of insignificance.
- Finally, you must take risks to create the life you desire.

*"Don't become one of the countless millions who've taken life's safe roads of indecision; that only leads to dead ends... disillusionment and disappointment.*

—NORMAN VINCENT PEALE

# 6

# LIVE BY INTEGRITY

Scriptures tell us that some men's sins are opened beforehand, and some remain for judgment. I'm in that first group. Anytime I've sinned by getting off track with my integrity, God has immediately corrected me. Here's an example:

It was a Saturday afternoon. Judy, Jason, Josh, and I had just left the Auburndale flea market. That's when I spotted an old Ford Econoline pickup on a used car lot nearby. It was one of those little butt-nose service trucks used as service trucks by GTE (General Telephone & Electric), Sears, and others. I immediately decided to buy the truck. While I was negotiating the deal, Judy and the boys drove back home.

Then it happened. The used car dealer said, "There's no need to pay sales tax on the full selling price. I'll show the sales price lower; you'll still pay the original amount, but I'll show the price as $200 less, plus tax."

I didn't think I was cheating the state. He was. I

shouldn't have agreed to let him do that, but I did. How did God correct me?

On the way home, the right front wheel and tire ran off, and the right front of the Econoline quickly fell to the ground. The wrecker charged me $500 to tow the little truck to my home. On a positive note, I kept that little truck for fifteen years and even restored it a couple of times, eventually restoring it as an old-time Coca-Cola Truck.

To earn the trust and respect of others, integrity is paramount! Your integrity is the adherence to core principles. Without trust, nothing else matters! Trust thrives in an environment of mutual awareness. Therefore, ensure everyone involved is on the same page, as this creates mutual expectations. Mutual expectations are critical for the survival of meaningful relationships and any healthy organization.

Ethics cannot be compartmentalized. There's no such thing as 'business ethics,' 'personal ethics,' 'Christian ethics', etc. Who you are is not dependent upon where you live or work or what you do. There's no gray area when it comes to ethics. You're either an ethical person or you're not. Period.

*"Your integrity is the foundation upon which all your other values are built."*

—Brian Tracey

Trust and respect are the lynchpins that create an organization's working environment. As the leader, your example is what others look to. Remember, the speed of the leader determines the speed of the team. Open and honest dialogue creates an environment of trust. Honest dialogue provides mutual awareness, which is necessary for any relationship to thrive. Ensure that all those involved who need to know are aware and on the same page. Whenever things don't go as planned, it will help everyone to understand and accept what you share as the truth. This will improve everyone's perception of you as being honest and knowledgeable, i.e., your trustworthiness.

Today, social media, TV, entertainment, AI, and internet blogs are the shapers of society's values. Fifty years ago, it was the church and Scripture.

*"We set young leaders up for a fall if we encourage them to envision what they could do before they consider the kind of person they should become."*

—RUTH BARTON

# REVIEW

- Open and honest communication is vital to understand each other. Practice integrity to ensure there's trust in your relationships.
- Your integrity is the trait people rely upon when choosing whether to trust you.
- All things being equal, people prefer to deal with someone they trust. Are you trustworthy? When things are no longer equal, people would rather deal with someone they trust and respect. With integrity, you'll be trusted and respected.
- Keep promises. Do what you said you'd do. Do what's expected and more.
- Consider the best interests of others, and you're more apt to exercise integrity.
- Put borders around your lifestyle to safeguard your integrity. Surround yourself with wise counsel. Respect and listen to their views and recommendations.
- Be willing to admit your mistakes. People see your transparency as a sign of strength, not weakness.
- Regaining lost trust is far more costly than any short-term losses you may experience by doing the right thing in the first place.
- When a culture's values conflict with what you hold as truth, it creates a dilemma, forcing you to choose between them. Of course, cultural influencers are doing their best to desensitize us. Always default to the truth, always.
- Your self-discipline and authenticity are the lynchpins of your integrity.

*"What we do on some great occasion will likely depend on who we already are, and who we are will be the result of daily practicing integrity and self-discipline."*

—Henry Parry Liddon, English Theologian

# 7

# DEVELOP YOUR INFLUENCE

*"Your gifts alone won't make you amazing. However, when your gifts are coupled with God's anointing, your influence will become amazing."*

—John C. Maxwell, Author, Speaker, and Leadership Trainer

As I've shared in a previous chapter, my life began as the seventh child of South Georgia sharecroppers. Therefore, my family never owned a home or land.

We only farmed land for landowners, known as Landlords. We usually moved to a different farm every year because Daddy was always looking for an honest landlord who would pay him better. Landlords were glad to provide a rickety old house for us to live in while farming their land because Daddy was a hardworking farmer who brought along extra low-wage workers…seven of us young 'uns. Daddy's 'share' of the crop's profits at year-end was usually only enough to pay off bills accumulated at the local grocery store and fertilizer supplier. Therefore, I decided early on that farming was not for me. Yet, I'm thankful for the character and influence I learned from Daddy. He was an honest, trustworthy, hardworking man. He also demonstrated integrity by showing me that a man's word is his bond, a principle I've always followed. When his life neared the end, he called me aside and shared these powerful words:

*"Son, I don't have anything valuable to leave you, but hopefully, my influence will prove valuable in your life. And, son, always remember, your influence is the only inheritance you'll leave that will last for all eternity."*

—CHARLIE V. DOBBS SR., AS QUOTED BY JOHN C. MAXWELL IN *BECOMING A PERSON OF INFLUENCE*

When your life is over, and there's slow walking and sad music, what will you be remembered for accomplishing in life? Take a few minutes and write two or three sentences of your ideal eulogy.

## This Scientist's Contributions Saved Tens of Thousands of Lives

The year was 1861. America was on the verge of a horrible Civil War. White farm owners Moses and Susan Carver were getting ready for bed when a group of crazed men, known as Quantrill's Raiders, rode onto their Missouri property with torches, screaming profanities, and shooting. They targeted this farm because black families, who were not slaves, were living on the white couple's property. The raiders burned the family's barn, shot several people, and dragged off a young black woman named Mary Washington, who refused to let go of her tiny infant son.

Moses Carver's wife, Susan, considered Mary her best friend, so Moses sent the word out immediately, hoping to arrange a meeting with the cutthroats.

Carver was trying his best to get Mary and her baby back. He even offered to trade his prized stallion for the return of Mary and her infant baby. Within a few days, a meeting was set. And on a frigid winter night, Moses Carver rode several hours to a dark crossroads in Northern Arkansas.

There, he met Quantrill's men. They arrived on horse-back carrying torches, wearing flour sacks with holes cut out over their heads. Carver dismounted and traded his prized horse for what they threw in a burlap bag.

As they thundered off, Moses peered into the burlap bag, fell to his knees, and wept. He began praying because he knew the baby's mother was already dead. He asked the Lord to keep the tiny baby alive.

In the freezing dark, he reached into the bag and brought out a cold, naked, almost dead baby boy. Opening his jacket and shirt, he placed the crying and freezing infant against his chest. Weeping, he then began the long walk back to his home in Diamond, Missouri.

Carver talked to the trembling and whimpering infant all the way home, telling him he would always be loved and cared for and that he'd now have the same last name as his. His name would now be George Washington Carver.

Today, it is estimated that over two billion lives worldwide have been saved because of the thousands of medical uses for plants and their extracts discovered by renowned scientist George Washington Carver and his young protégé, Henry Wallace, whom Carver groomed as his competent assistant.

This could not have happened without the sacrifice of Moses Carver, the man who braved crazy terrorists on a freezing night to rescue and adopt an infant whose life would have been thrown away. Like Moses Carver, your influence is also eternal. The truth is, you can create or change your influence for the better beginning now.

Ask yourself, "What difference will my life make?" Reflect on your current influence as it is today, and decide what to change for the better, one day, one act at a time.

It's life's challenges, not successes, which provide wisdom. We obtain wisdom by progressing through life's trials and challenges. Not so much from successes, as focusing on your accomplishments alone will tempt you to relax and rest on your laurels. It's important to remember that while your wisdom dies with you, your influence, especially what you teach others, will last for eternity.

> *Never underestimate the power of your influence. A good word, an Atta-boy, or an Atta-girl, a simple statement, a few words of encouragement, are valuable investments in the lives of those whom you influence."*
>
> — Angela Brown, Co-author of *Resilience* and founder of OmniMedia Consulting Group

When I was starting out, I tried to build a business that specialized in replacement parts for classic Mustangs.

My goal was to provide items Mustang enthusiasts would need to put the finishing touches on their Mustangs.

Since I didn't have deep pockets nor a warehouse full of parts and accessories for their restorations, I specialized in less costly items, i.e., owner's and shop manuals, decals, striping kits, the finishing touches they'd need to ensure every aspect of their freshly restored vehicle, would look just like it did when it rolled off the showroom floor.

I acquired most of the original decals affixed to various parts of the cars when they were new. Most originals had been sanded off or faded out. All these would need to be reapplied when the owner's restoration was complete. However, when I visited a local screen-printing company, I discovered that I would need to order several thousand of each decal or striping kit for them to be reproduced. I couldn't afford to order those large quantities.

Then, interestingly, one day, as I was eating lunch at the Reesecliff Restaurant on South Florida Avenue in Lakeland, I noticed that across the street was what appeared to be a renovated gas station that had been converted into a sign shop. The sign read, 'Dixie Signs.' I walked over, went inside, and met Mr. Leroy J. Douglass, the owner.

I asked if he could manufacture novelty license plates showing the model year of a Mustang's manufacture.

He said, "Sure, son, I can do that."

Then, I told him I would only need a few hundred of each decal.

He said, "No problem! I'm the CEO of Douglass Screen Printers, and since I'm the owner, they will create anything I want."

I then explained my dilemma to him regarding

getting his screen-printing company to reproduce the original Mustang decals and striping kits in small quantities, rather than thousands. That's when he looked out the window and saw my Ford Econoline van outside with large Mustang Club of America logos painted on the side.

He said, "Son, it looks like you're just starting out in business, and I'd like to help you. Let me call Tom, my president of Douglass Screen Printers."

I listened as he told Tom to have their company create and print anything I needed in whatever quantities I wanted and to do it at a reasonably low price.

I subsequently learned that Mr. Douglass was a wealthy Lakeland native and one of the founders of Lakeland's largest Christian schools. Lakeland Christian School is where my son, Jason, subsequently graduated.

## This Man Also had a Positive Influence on My Life and This Book

Years later, while teaching LifeSkills at my church, I asked fellow church board member and successful businessman Larry Maxwell if he would introduce me to his brother John C. Maxwell someday. At the time John C. Maxwell was pastoring a large church in San Diego, California, and had also authored numerous books on leadership.

Larry said he'd be glad to introduce me to his brother, John. He added, "Matter of fact, Larry, I'm picking John up at the Tampa Airport in a couple of hours. If you'd like, you can ride along."

I gladly agreed.

While having lunch that day with John, he asked me about my publishing company and other activities in which I was involved. I told him about my publishing company and the LifeSkills class I'd created.

John then asked what kind of hard-copy files (this was predigital) I kept on all the topical curriculum materials I was teaching, such as Encouragement, Determination, Passion, etc. Ashamedly, I said I wasn't keeping any hard files.

John then gave me the best advice ever for a writer or speaker. He told me to begin filing, by topic, any materials related to the specific classes I taught, and to also gather articles from magazines and newspaper stories for those files. He said this would become a treasure trove of material for the future.

Therefore, much of the content of this book is the result of that wise counsel that John C. Maxwell gave me that day, years ago, while we were at lunch. To this day, I often refer to those files. This was definitely pre-Artificial Intelligence.

Then, months later, John called me about a manuscript for a book he was writing, *Becoming a Person of Influence*. He asked me whether I had anything to say about influence to include in the book. I was honored to share the wisdom my daddy had offered me years earlier. John included Daddy's quote on influence in his new book.

Thus, I would be remiss if I didn't express my appreciation to John C. Maxwell for encouraging me to keep files of all my lessons and presentations.

## My Daily Prayer is to Be a Godly Influencer

*"O Lord, please give me opportunities today to positively influence the lives of those I encounter."*

Perhaps you know someone whose influence elicits this response? "He brightens up the room...just by leaving." Don't be that guy.

# R E V I E W

- Create an influence and reputation of reliability and trustworthiness.
- Spend quality time thinking about your influence and what actions are needed to improve it. In doing so, you will also improve your career resume.
- Your resume validates what you have done or can do and your competence, while your legacy will reveal the difference you've made in the lives of others. Your influence is key to creating a meaningful legacy.
- People will be more open and honest when you practice the powerful communication skill of listening with understanding. Not with solutions!
- Share a pleasant smile to spread hope and encouragement. This will also convey calm assurance about you.
- Have a goal to put people at ease around you. They'll be more likely to be attracted to you and more likely to look forward to being in your presence.
- As a leader, when correction is needed, do so privately and couple corrections with words of appreciation and encouragement.
- Those you influence will often seek to become the person your encouragement and expectations inspired them to become. So, start today by being that positive influence in another's life.

# 8

# COMMUNICATE EFFECTIVELY

*"People want to be with people who make them feel special, not people who try to convince others they're the one who's special. Take responsibility to help the people you talk with feel as if they're the only person in the room."*

—DEBRA FINE, AUTHOR AND
COMMUNICATIONS TRAINER

ONE WEEKEND, WE were relocating Dobbs Publishing Group's corporate offices to a beautiful new building. All my employees worked hard to finish the move over the weekend. That's when I saw one of them putting items in the wrong office. I immediately verbally corrected her. She was both embarrassed and offended, and she let me know it. Her verbal response not only expressed her disappointment with my scolding words, but she also helped me to understand that my blunt, corrective actions were inappropriate and out of line.

She told me that if I wasn't pleased with where

she'd put the items, I should have said so privately, not harshly correcting her in front of all the other employees. Additionally, she suggested that as the company's senior leader, I should consider taking classes on effective communication. I felt about two inches tall and apologized within earshot of those who'd witnessed our terse conversation. The following week. I signed up for Stephen Covey's "Seven Habits of Highly Effective People" seminar. A wise choice, as I certainly needed improvement in my communication skills.

Thereafter, I paid for many of the employees on my leadership team, including myself, to attend seminars and workshops led by Stephen Covey, Dale Carnegie, and Marshall Goldsmith. Some would say that was a very costly expenditure. Yes, but the improvement in my team's ability to become better communicators made it a worthwhile investment.

## God Chose to Equip and Anoint a Boy

As a five-year-old, he was excited as he listened to the speaker's words. His daddy was proud of how well the little fellow listened to the preacher. The boy saw that others in the crowd were listening too. Wouldn't it be great to have people listening to me speak? Maybe someday.

As a teenager, he attended Florida Bible Institute. The boy still wanted to become someone who could captivate people with his words. He then began pursuing his own emerging talents to preach anywhere possible. The swampy area surrounding the Tampa campus offered a reasonable audience. Oh yes, from alligators to birds, he'd paddle his canoe out to a small island and preach to all the creatures great and small. No animals were converted, but he didn't stop sharing his message.

Friends and family said he was a good listener, but didn't think he was a very good speaker.

As a college student, his greatest ambition was to preach at the West Tampa Gospel Mission. The mission was in that city's Hispanic district. He thought, What are the chances of that ever happening?

Then, one day, as he was passing the mission, he decided to stop and pray about getting a chance to speak in the mission. So, he kneeled and prayed aloud right then.

When he stood up, he was startled that the fellow who ran the mission was standing there.

The man said, "I heard your prayer, son. Our scheduled speaker for tomorrow had to cancel. Could you fill in for him?"

Astonished by such an immediate answer to his prayer, he nodded. He often remembered that pivotal moment as a tremendous faith builder in his life and ministry.

The mission director was so impressed by the young man's message and communication skills that the invitation was reissued many times. Every weekend, he refined his message, and his communication skills became even more anointed and convincing. He preached to anyone who would gather. Soon, his presentation and speaking ability grew more powerful.

After college, he took his ministry on the road. He'd travel from town to town, often preaching on temporary stages. Sometimes in tents and in any church that offered him a pulpit…He built his reputation one community at a time. Yet, gaining national prominence seemed very distant to the young man.

Then, one day, a little grandmother heard him speak and thought everybody needed to hear this message. Although she had never met the young man before, she did what a spirit-filled grandmother is apt to do. She picked up the phone and dialed information for the home phone number of Randolph Hearst, the world's most powerful newspaper magnate at the time.

What are the chances that multi-billionaire Randolph Hearst would answer the phone? He did!

She said, "Now, you listen to me, Mr. Hearst. I've just heard the most powerful speaker I've ever heard, and you need to tell the world about him. They need to hear his message!"

Mr. Hearst got the young man's name and immediately called his company's secretary to investigate. He liked what he heard about the young man and his message.

Then he instructed his secretary to send telegrams to the hundreds of editors of all the Hearst Newspapers, telling them to begin promoting this young man in their newspapers as someone whose message could make a difference in the world.

Within a few days, the name Billy Graham was known worldwide. In his lifetime, hundreds of millions heard his powerful, anointed messages and came to faith!

I created this communication acrostic for relationship workshops I taught to business executives, couples, and individuals wishing to improve their relationship skills:

## The Keys to My Heart:

**H** ear me with understanding, not solutions.

**E** ncourage me, even when I fail.

**A** ffirm me for who I am.

**R** espect me with honor.

**T** rust me and be trustworthy.

Remember these five simple letters to become a more effective communicator.

# REVIEW

*"What sets great communicators apart? For them, there's no on-off switch for caring, empathy, and showing respect. The switch is always on."*

—MARSHALL GOLDSMITH, AUTHOR OF *WHAT GOT YOU HERE WON'T GET YOU THERE*

- Wise men speak because they have something to say. Fools speak because they have to say something.
- Practice listening with understanding. Don't be judgmental, and don't jump to solutions. Refuse to interrupt. Be patient. Don't press them for the bottom line.
- Want to be a more interesting person? Then, get others talking about themselves and what's happening in their lives. Once they feel understood, they're more apt to want to hear your views and opinions.
- Great communicators maintain eye contact, and they don't glance around. Silence your phone. Avoid getting involved in other activities. Become all ears, hear their whole story, and let them finish. Turn off any screens and focus on them.
- Train yourself in the art of asking questions instead of offering solutions and giving instructions. Ask reflective questions and express understanding. This does not mean you agree with their opinions.
- Remember: the speaker's facts might be flawed,

but their feelings are valid. Thus, ask questions about the facts instead of challenging their feelings. Remember, his or her feelings are what matter most to the speaker.

- Great communicators have learned the difficult art of suspending certainty. Be willing to suspend certainty (judgment) if your goal is to understand what the person is feeling based on what they're saying. Remember, they're looking for understanding more than agreement.

- Don't feel challenged by questions; they simply want more information. So, remain calm as you answer their questions.

*"The three main things we look for in a friend are someone who'll listen, offer understanding, and validate our feelings."*

—Scott Stanley, Minirth Meier Clinic

# 9
# RESOLVE CONFLICT

*"If you always want to be in charge, learn to be a ringmaster. If you want to be in a meaningful relationship, learn to resolve conflict."*

—LARRY G. DOBBS

GOT PEOPLE? GOT conflict! Learning to resolve conflict is essential for lasting, fulfilling relationships. Otherwise, you'll spend your time arguing, fighting, or fleeing. Don't be fooled. Unresolved conflict always resurfaces as resentment, which, if not addressed, will become bitterness or even hatred.

I'll confess I didn't want to write this chapter. Conflict resolution is not my strength. I'd considered this LifeSkills book complete, but while sitting at our table recently with our son Nathan, he said something that caused me to rethink whether the book was complete. We were discussing what's needed for a healthy relationship. He said earlier in his and Jenna's marriage that they were going through tough times and under a lot of stress. As Christians, they wanted to become the loving, caring couple they'd dreamed of becoming when they first married. So, they sought professional counsel. The following is Nathan's recount of one of their counseling sessions.

"Jenna and I were in the marriage counselor's office, and the session was about over, when the counselor abruptly said, 'Nathan, I don't think I've ever counseled anyone who had an IQ as high as yours…and an EQ as low as yours.' I was aghast. Why is my emotional quotient so low if I'm highly intelligent?"

Then, Nathan shared the good news of their relationship. He said, thankfully, today, he and Jenna are doing great relationally, spiritually, and financially, feeling happy and blessed. Why? Because they focused on improving their Emotional Intelligence, largely relying upon God's Holy Spirit to help them. Nathan says that with God's help, they have accomplished emotionally what they could not achieve intellectually. Nathan said they've learned to understand the basic differences between their emotional quotient (EQ) and their intelligence quotient (IQ).

## AI Web Browser PERPLEXITY Defines IQ and EQ Differences:

*IQ assesses cognitive abilities like logical reasoning, problem-solving, and knowledge retention. IQ is often innate and linked to academic success.*

*EQ evaluates emotional intelligence, including self-awareness, empathy, and social skills. EQ is learned and reflects one's ability to manage emotions and relationships effectively.*

*While IQ aids intellectual tasks, EQ is crucial for interpersonal interactions. Both are complementary and valuable in personal and professional success.*

Author and psychologist Scott Stanley states he can predict with 95% accuracy whether a marriage relationship will last based on how well the couple handles conflict. Having a business with seventy-five highly intelligent employees, I discovered that the statistics are similar in the workplace. As a matter of fact, I've often seen that unhappiness transcends all a person's relationships, whether at work, at home, or in the community.

Relationship experts claim the best time to address conflict is now. The longer you put off resolving the conflict, the worse it will become and the more difficult it will be to reach a resolution.

**Warning:** The resentment resulting from unresolved conflict becomes Satan's main tool for destroying your relationships. Unresolved conflict does not die. Burying your feelings is not the solution. The bad feelings will resurface, only uglier and worse.

*"The surest ticket to slavery is the resentment brought about by unresolved conflict. If you hold onto resentment against a person, the person is with you when you eat, when you sleep."*

—Clergyman John Powell

The common denominator in conflict is people. Yet, we all need people. What's required to resolve conflict, and how do we avoid it? What do "Once upon a time" and "They lived happily ever after" have in common? Both are fairy tales. The current failure rate of approximately fifty percent of marriages is evidence of unresolved conflict in society. Being a member of those statistics, I speak from experience.

I'm thankful that my commitment to learning to better handle conflict has enabled me to be happily married. And I've discovered that being in a fulfilling relationship requires you to be willing to ask God to empower you with humility by His Holy Spirit. I tried being married without God, but my failure was further proof that the chances of a stable, fulfilling marriage without God are not good.

God created mankind with an innate need for other people. The lyrics of a popular 1960s song by Simon & Garfunkel. "I am a Rock; I am an Island" reflected emotional isolation and self-protection, being self-centered, alone, and detached. Therefore, unless you want to become a hermit or a sad and lonely curmudgeon, be willing to learn how to improve your ability to resolve conflicts. Review the twelve conflict resolution tips on the next page before beginning any controversial discussions arising from conflict.

# R E V I E W

## Helpful Tips to Resolve Conflict

1.  Begin your discussion with prayer, asking God to direct your conversation.
2.  Be aware that conflict is the best arena for observing one's character.
3.  Set time limits by allocating time increments for participants and ensure the time allocated works for all involved.
4.  Your relationships are more important than the issues being discussed.
5.  Your life is comprised of tasks and relationships. However, remember, relationships are your life's most important tasks.
6.  Be humble and sincere, giving priority to your relationship with those involved.
7.  Listen attentively to each other's viewpoints, with the goal of understanding one another's feelings.
8.  Try to be humble but with focused sincerity, as this is your best strategy for disarming anger.
9.  When the conversation gets too heated, consider taking a 10-minute time-out.
10. Avoid profanity and vulgarity, as animosity will lead to everyone losing control.
11. Never attack or discount another's feelings. Their facts might be flawed, but their feelings are real.
12. Successfully resolving conflict requires that the goal is not to have a winner or loser. Rather, the goal is to restore harmony in your relationship.

# 10
# ADAPT TO CHANGE

*"Your life does not improve by chance; it only gets better by changing."*

— JIM ROHN

MY LIFE'S DIRECTION dramatically changed as a young man when I saw her walking by, wearing a snappy red pantsuit with cute little plastic elephants as the waist belt buckle. I was smitten! So, I asked her boss, my friend, Bill, for her name. He told me her name but also told me not to try to get to know her. Because she was a senior at Southeastern Bible College and a preacher's daughter from South Georgia, Bill said her parents wanted her to become a missionary.

Little did they know that I'd be her first mission. It wasn't long before I asked her out, and thankfully, she said yes! We went out a few times before she learned my checkered backstory. Being a Christian young woman, she went to her pastor for advice about dating a divorced guy who drank, smoked, and used profanity. I was not a Christian. Her pastor counseled her, telling her that there were two chances I would ever change my lifestyle. Slim and none. She called me and broke up. Bummer!

The following Sunday, both upset and curious, I attended her church. She saw me but purposefully ignored me. The following Sunday, I wasn't sure why, but I was back at her church. That time, at the close of the pastor's sermon, I had an unusual feeling inside. I left, not knowing God's Holy Spirit was drawing me to Christ to change my way of living. Another Sunday, I felt compelled to return to her church. When the pastor's sermon message ended, I walked immediately down the center aisle and knelt at the church's altar in tears, asking God for forgiveness for my sinful lifestyle. Miraculously, God's Holy Spirit began changing how I acted and lived. Christians refer to this as coming to faith or getting saved, also called a conversion, which means converting from non-believers to believers.

I began living very differently. In my heart, I knew that my life was going to be different. However, my two roommates thought I'd gone off the deep end since I no longer wanted to party, carouse, and drink with them.

It was quite a while before Judy would go out with me again because she wasn't sure my conversion was genuine. Thankfully, after some time, she became convinced that God had truly changed my life. Then, after we had dated for several months, I asked her to marry me. She said yes!

After marrying Judy, I realized that I needed to establish goals for my life. We all make mistakes; however, you're going in reverse if you're making the same mistakes year after year. That described what I'd been doing.

I knew I needed to change personally. I also needed to change professionally and spiritually as my life rapidly changed. It's called sanctification. The Holy Spirit was busy at work, getting my life in order.

Judy's parents and family, however, did not favor our marriage. As a matter of fact, it was a few years before I was accepted. The Holy Spirit helped me to be patient and trust God, to help Judy's family to see the difference my coming to faith had made in my life. Thankfully, after we'd been married for a while, they finally saw my faith and lifestyle change was real.

God has a sense of humor because years later, He created an event that helped my relationship improve. Judy's parents came to our home unexpectedly to visit for the weekend. On a Friday evening, I received a call from my friend, retired Assembly of God pastor Jack Carrier. Jack and I were collectors of various memorabilia. We often chatted and did some collectibles trading.

Jack said he was calling because his good friend, Assembly of God, National Superintendent, Tom Trask, had flown into town for the weekend, and that Tom would like to come over and ride in my Lingenfelter Corvette. The late John Lingenfelter of Lingenfelter Performance Engineering built the car as a project for one of my magazines, *Corvette Fever*. The car had nearly 800 horsepower and was extremely fast! I told Jack to bring Reverend Trask over, and we'd go for a ride.

It's important to note that Judy's dad, 96 years old as of this writing, is a lifelong Assembly of God pastor and the builder of numerous churches nationwide. He also has an investment company that finances church construction projects.

I then asked Judy's dad, the Reverend Shelvie Summerlin Sr., if he'd ever met Reverend Tom Trask. He said he hadn't. I asked if he would like to meet him.

He said he'd like to meet the General Superintendent but doubted he'd ever get the opportunity to meet him.

I proudly said, "You'll get to meet him in a few minutes. He's on the way over here." That opportunity to introduce Judy's dad to the Assemblies of God's General Superintendent made me feel a bit smug.

As was Reverend Trask's tradition with everyone he met, he gave Judy's dad a godly kiss on the cheek when he left. I believe introducing Reverend Summerlin to Reverend Trask gave me a bit more credibility with Judy's dad. I thought, God, you did this!

The key is that we must be willing to change. It could be the difference between your success and failure in life. In business, finance, and ministry, change is required.

Few of the 500 largest companies of a century ago are still around. Those that remain have had to drastically change during the past century. For example, during our lifetime, book publishers' long-term goal was to sell books to bookstores. The internet changed that. As a matter of fact, almost all businesses and organizations have totally changed in my lifetime and yours.

Change is the only constant. Many now-defunct companies, like Sears, Circuit City, Montgomery Wards, Woolworths, Blockbuster, Encyclopedia Britannica, and hundreds of others, got stuck in the past. They struggled but failed to survive. Why? Because they were unable or unwilling to change. Are you listening?

*"Wisdom is the reward you get for a lifetime of empathic listening, especially in those times when you would have preferred to talk."*

—Doug Larson

Are you currently doing what God and you had intended? Did you know that Adolph Hitler felt called to be an artist? As a teenager, he told his parents he felt called to be an artist. So, at the age of eighteen, he took his inheritance, seven hundred kronen, and moved to Vienna to live and study art. Records reveal that he applied to the Academy of Fine Arts and later to the School of Architecture. Have you ever seen one of Hitler's paintings? You won't because he never began doing what God intended. He procrastinated. His life's misguided purpose soon became Satan's workshop, and millions of lives were lost.

# REVIEW

*"Without the willingness to change, you cannot expect anything to be different this year than it was last year. The default in your life will always be more of the same."*

—PASTOR RICK WARREN

- When electricity came along, a swath of industries became trapped in their old way of thinking. The survivors were willing to walk away from what they used to do to embrace a new way of thinking.
- Ask yourself, "How is my life different today than it was five or ten years ago?"
- What research have you done, or books have you read this year, related to your career and the latest advancements?
- What seminars or workshops have you attended recently to become more knowledgeable about the changes in your career field?
- Decide which LifeSkills you will improve this year. Changing for the better is the difference your life will make.

*"The thief comes only to steal, kill, and destroy. I have come in order that you might have life—life in all its fullness."*

(JOHN 10:10, THE GOOD NEWS TRANSLATION)

# 11

# CREATE YOUR LIFE PLAN

*"Create your plan and reduce it to writing…the moment you do, you'll give concrete form to your desired results; you'll now have a roadmap for a successful journey."*

—Napoleon Hill

When I launched a start-up niche business called Mustang Supply Company, my goal was to sell parts and accessories for early Mustangs. This included any dated NOS (New Old Stock) parts I could find in stockrooms and warehouses of Ford auto dealers, as well as original factory literature, shop manuals, owner's manuals, etc., related to the cars. Since Mr. Douglass had been so kind as to allow me to recreate and reproduce the various factory decals, labels, and striping kits, I also created a wholesale network for volume sales to other suppliers catering to Mustang enthusiasts.

My plan was working. The business was doing well. However, due to my experience in marketing, I knew the real opportunity would be to create a medium for the tens of thousands of enthusiasts and dealers to buy, sell, and trade parts, accessories, and vehicles. Since I was an experienced newspaper advertising salesman, I created a monthly classified newsletter for Mustang enthusiasts.

In December of that year, I bought a full-page advertisement in *Hemmings Motor News*, a successful classified advertising magazine with several hundred thousand readers and subscribers nationwide. The cost of that full-page advertisement was almost $800. Ninety-two Mustang enthusiasts sent in $7 checks. A total of $644. A difference of well over a hundred dollars. However, I was not discouraged by the deficit.

The response proved my belief that there was enough interest in a monthly classified newsletter and that these subscribers would spread the word to fellow Mustang enthusiasts. My belief was correct. Without further advertising, the following month, over 200 new subscriptions came in the mail, along with more than fifty phone-in requests, asking for an invoice for the cost. That's when I decided to offer these respondents the opportunity to subscribe for two years at $14 or three years at $21. Most opted for three years. At that time, postage and quick printing were very inexpensive, so I was off to a small yet profitable start-up.

By today's standards, it wasn't impressive, but I believed I was onto something bigger. In future years, with continual growth in circulation and advertising. *Mustang Monthly Magazine* remained my number one revenue producer of all the magazines I published for the next twenty years.

Marketing experts claim that the original product, or

first magazine, is seldom overtaken by later competitors. No other Mustang magazine overtook *Mustang Monthly* during my twenty years of owning it.

It's best to take the vital steps of research and planning before beginning. A valid business plan provides a roadmap to follow and is also essential if you hope to obtain third-party or outside financing.

Caution: Don't become so enthusiastic about achieving your goals that you forget to take the important step of creating a detailed action plan, or you're sure to get off course right from the get-go. Harried busyness will not replace a detailed plan of action that's created by deep thinking and wise counsel. Numerous studies have shown that one of the major reasons businesses and organizations fail is poor planning or a lack of planning. Taking unplanned risks can be fun, but they are seldom reliable.

# REVIEW

- Wise planning includes calculating what's known and what's realistically expected through market research. Your plan will guide you to stay on track.

- Begin by creating and writing a rough draft of your overall plan. Then, edit and refine it into step-by-step goals. Build in flexibility, allowing for the unexpected, which is sure to occur.

- Truthfully evaluate whether you're currently pre-pared financially, personally, and professionally to begin this new life journey. Progress requires preparation.

- Your plan provides a future to believe in, something to look forward to.

- Have the wisdom and humility to sit down and engage in meaningful conversation with those who'll accompany you on this journey. This will make the trip far more pleasant for all involved.

- Learn to be proactive if you hope to be successful. Show up every day, put one foot in front of the other, and do the work needed. Studies reveal that showing up and doing the work, day by day makes the difference in success.

# 12

# STAY RELEVANT

*"That which you nurture thrives; that which you neglect dies."*

— Dr. Crandall Miller

As soon as Dobbs Publishing Group began growing and becoming profitable, I realized I still had much to learn about the publishing business.

About that time, Joshua, our second child, was born. Judy then decided to stay at home with our two young children. Today, I'm blessed that our three sons, Jason, Joshua, and Melody's son, Nathan, are successful Christian adults. We're very proud of them.

Soon, because of my success as a niche publisher, I decided I also wanted to stand out, not be just a small-market publisher. Thus, I began improving my direct-mail marketing and copywriting skills, attending seminars and workshops related to the large-market publishing industry. I traveled from NYC to New Orleans, San Francisco to LA., seeking to learn as much as possible about direct mail and copyrighting. I always try to learn as much as possible to stay relevant in the magazine publishing industry.

One of the key professionals I sought counsel from was the late and great Renee' Gnam. Renee' was the guru of direct mail marketing at the time. I met him at a publishing seminar in New York City. I was very impressed with his one-hour presentation, so I got his phone number and learned he lived in Tarpon Springs, Florida, only about two hours from where I live. When I got home, I called him to ask about his daily consulting rates. OMG! I was shocked. I asked if he ever offered hourly consulting. He was gracious, realizing I was a small publisher who lived nearby. Small compared to the mega-bucks' publishers he did consulting and direct mail packages for.

Renee told me to bring my notepad and pen to his ranch in Tarpon Springs, and he'd meet with me and answer any questions I had about direct marketing for $1,000 for a half-day. I gladly agreed and set up an appointment. I can truthfully say that's perhaps the best thousand dollars I've ever spent. I filled six notebook pages with questions and answers. The major publishers paid upwards of $50,000-$100,000 for Renee to write one direct mail package. He said I was an anomaly to seek his services like I did. Yet, it was my way of learning all I could about writing and creating successful direct mail packages.

Soon, I stood out as a knowledgeable publisher and marketer. This was one of the main reasons the big publishers wanted to purchase my company. They wanted to know what we were doing to grow successfully. Quite simply, my strategy was to seek wise counsel and always do the right thing in the right way and at the right time.

## Why Being a 'Standout' is Essential for Achieving Your Dreams

In today's culture, everyone is pressured to fit in. However, if your goal is to excel, choose instead to stand out by being a continual learner. The great influencers in history were individuals who seldom fit in. They stood out because they took risks, tried something new, and were not afraid of failing. Steve Jobs and Steve Wozniak were scorned by their peers when they planned to create the first Apple Computer, but that wasn't the market they were catering to. Thomas Edison failed numerous times before finally creating electric lighting. Learning and creativity go hand in hand. Elon Musk was laughed out of the offices of major automobile manufacturers when he approached them about his Tesla vision.

Those who courageously step out to pursue their dream of making a difference are seldom cheered on by critics because culture prefers that you fit in, not stand out. Don't allow culture to pigeonhole you. Begin where you are today, choosing to become a lifelong learner.

Remember, life is a teacher, and lifelong learners advance more quickly. Whenever you choose to be a learner, you'll discover your life is filled with hope.

Commit to doing what's needed for success, day after day. Statistics prove that eighty percent of success comes from committing yourself to show up day after day and doing the work to the best of your ability. Opportunities are only available to those who are on track, showing up daily, and doing the work.

# REVIEW

- Statistically, after midlife, most people accept their life position and cease learning and growing. Steven Alistad, a leading expert on aging and author of the book *Why We Age,* says 75% of what determines individual longevity is an active lifestyle, including a commitment to learning and growth.

- The danger of stopping learning and growing is becoming complacent. Soon, you'll lose interest in anything worthy of importance. Then, your mind becomes firmly set like concrete. Thereafter, you'll have a mindset that's unable to be stirred.

- However, be encouraged because when you choose to continue learning and growing, you will control much of your longevity, expanding your life's possibilities.

- Having more control will require you to stay relevant. Staying relevant means you don't have the attitude of a know-it-all, thinking you don't need to learn anything new.

- Life is your teacher; as a lifelong learner, you'll advance much farther and more quickly.

- With the advent and proliferation of AI (Artificial Intelligence), you must become a lifelong learner. List what new technology skills you need to learn.

- Technology is currently doubling every two years. Plus, with the advent of AI (Artificial Intelligence), it's essential that you stay relevant and current.

# 13

# PREPARE FOR OBSTACLES

When life is challenging, we're apt to learn the most—if we're listening. Wisdom is the reward you get for a lifetime of listening when you would have preferred talking.

I was a young, happily married man when I got a call from my sister telling me our mother had terminal cancer. For the next few weeks, Judy and I drove to Georgia to be with Mother. Too soon, she passed away.

That was a sad time. However, things got worse quickly. For weeks, I had been suffering from a severe tonsillitis infection. Sickness wasn't normal for me; I was a healthy young guy who seldom got ill. Doctors later speculated that the tonsil infection had triggered a chronic autoimmune illness. Autoimmune is when your body's immune cells begin attacking your body's healthy cells. The grief of losing my mother, coupled with the tonsil infection, likely triggered autoimmune issues. I was rapidly losing weight, had an insatiable appetite, and had to urinate quite frequently. My wife, Judy, told me to go to the doctor.

I told her I'd be fine. But I wasn't.

The following week, as I made sales calls to my list of newspaper advertisers, my vision became blurry. So, I went to the hospital's emergency clinic. The on-call doctor did a glucose tolerance test and told me I had juvenile diabetes. Juvenile diabetes is now known as Type 1 diabetes. Confused, I asked him what diabetes was.

He said, "Well, son, unless you learn how to manage it, you'll probably be blind in five years. If you're lucky, you might live another ten years." The only advice he gave me was not to drink or eat sweets or potatoes. Not a good doctor!

The following week, my symptoms got worse. I went back to the emergency clinic. That day, the on-call ER doctor referred me to Dr. Eugene Davidson, a Primary Care doctor and widely recognized Endocrinologist at the Watson Clinic in Lakeland, Florida. After examining me, Dr. Davidson immediately admitted me to the hospital. There, Brenda, his diabetes educator, taught Judy and me how to give multiple daily injections of insulin, using a grapefruit as the recipient instead of me. This was before the creation of insulin pumps, continuous glucose monitors, and today's advanced medical technology.

After getting my diabetes within range, Dr. Davidson challenged me, saying that if I did what he instructed, I'd likely outlive him. I promised to follow his instructions. Back then, the only way to check whether I had too much sugar in my body was to put my urine in a vial, drop a tablet in the vial, and if it turned orange, it meant I had too much sugar in my body.

And I've continued doing as Dr. Davidson advised me for the last fifty years, thus, I'm still alive. Apparently,

God wants me to continue learning what my life will make possible. Sadly, my medical hero, Dr. Eugene Davidson, passed away a few years ago.

Living with a chronic illness is never easy. Some days, I'm doing okay; some days, it's overwhelming trying to balance insulin, carbohydrates, and exercise. Less than 10% of the millions of diabetics are Type 1 diabetics, like me. More than 90% are Type 2. The main difference between the two types of diabetics is that Type 2 diabetics can often manage their diabetes with a proper diet, exercise, and weight control. Some will require oral medication, and others will also require insulin.

All of us who are Type 1 must always have insulin, or we'll die. Eating honey, cinnamon, or any magic elixir that you see recommended online won't do it! To survive, we must have insulin continuously, as long as we live!

Medical science has been trying to find a cure for more than a century after four Canadian doctors, Fredrick Banting, Charles Best, J.J. Macleod, and J.B. Collip, discovered insulin in 1921. Insulin helps Type 1 diabetics manage their diabetes to survive. But, as of this writing, there is no cure, but we're making progress. Stem cell therapy has shown promise in managing Type 1 diabetes, but that is still under research.

Please know you can't CONTROL a chronic illness, only MANAGE it.

In those times when I become discouraged trying to manage this illness, I reflect on what the Apostle Paul dealt with in the Holy Bible. Scripture doesn't specify the chronic condition Paul was plagued with, but says he asked God on three different occasions to take away his chronic condition. Yet, God told Paul:

*"My grace is sufficient for you, for my power is made perfect in weakness."*

(2 Corinthians 12:9 New International Version)

Nevertheless, God reminds me of the meaningful accomplishments I've experienced in life, which have all been AFTER contracting this chronic illness, type-1 diabetes, fifty years ago. Therefore, I'm encouraged and will never give up!

Throughout my life, God has helped me become a successful magazine publisher and build a multi-million-dollar business. He has also allowed me to become a respected servant leader in my local church and community. I credit His goodness, grace, and anointing for choosing a once spiritually lost high school dropout with a chronic illness to accomplish success.

# R E V I E W

- It's wise to have a family, friends, and a spiritual network when life throws you a curve, bringing unexpected pressure and disappointment.
- Managing life's unexpected events also requires faith and determination. Having the courage to accept, learn, and adapt to life's unexpected happenings.
- Asking, "Why me?" is okay. Just be prepared for crickets instead of a quick answer. God is more concerned with your willingness to trust Him to provide the courage and strength rather than making your situation easier. Building your character is more important to God than creating your comfort.
- It's when life's difficult times arise that we must rely on friends and family whom He's blessed us with. God's strength and courage are most often provided through the hands of our loved ones.
- The unexpected can manifest itself in any number of ways. For me, these included losing my loving wife of thirty years and living fifty years with the chronic illness of type-1 diabetes. Nevertheless, I choose to continue, in faith, believing that God has a bright future for the remainder of my life.
- If your situation is a medical issue, have the discipline to follow the advice of savvy medical providers. Being a type-1 diabetic requires me to eat a healthy, balanced diet, exercise regularly, and get adequate rest. I must also be connected to an

insulin pump and a continuous glucose monitor (CGM).

- Additionally, if your medical condition requires you to see your healthcare professionals regularly, do so.
- Remember, you, the patient, are the best advocate for your healthcare.
- The bottom line is to never give up! Get up and try again those times when you fail. Determine to always fail forward.

# 14

# OVERCOME SETBACKS

This chapter is an overview of my business story.

My business began as a small operation with a quick-print newsletter on my kitchen table, and it eventually grew into a multi-million-dollar automotive magazine publishing company. My success stemmed from passion, determination, and the support of talented individuals willing to join me on this journey. It evolved into a company that I sold for over thirty times its annual earnings.

What started as an automotive hobby grew into a passion for Mustangs and expanded to include other American performance cars. In time, this passion enabled me to discover and accomplish the amazing possibilities that God enabled for my life.

## Starting a Mustang business: Serendipity or God-ordained?

I was a retail advertising salesman for the local newspaper. One morning, across the employee parking lot, I saw a

Springtime yellow 1965 Mustang convertible with a sign, 'Must Sell, only $250.00.' I walked over for a closer look. The keys were in the ignition, so I fired up the engine. It had seen better days. The floorboards were rusty, and the car's 289-cubic-inch V-8 engine was smoking badly. This ten-year-old Mustang really needed lots of work. Yet, I thought it had potential. I negotiated the young lady's price down to $200 cash.

Next began the laborious process of resurrecting that old Mustang convertible. Doing so helped spawn my knowledge and passion for early Mustangs.

Months later, the amateur restoration project was finally completed. The following weekend, my wife, Judy, and I drove our refurbished, thirteen-year-old Mustang from Lakeland, Florida, to Stone Mountain, Georgia, for a long weekend getaway. We arrived late Friday evening and checked into the Stone Mountain Inn. Looking out the hotel window Saturday morning, I noticed a gathering of Mustangs in the parking lot below.

After breakfast, we walked outside to see what was going on. Ironically, we learned this was the very first annual meeting of the Mustang Club of America. We walked around looking at all the Mustangs displayed and vendors with new and used parts and accessories for Mustangs. A young man named Gary was there, representing the newly organized Mustang Club of America. He encouraged me to join their club. I became member #229.

Later, while driving back to Florida, I commented to Judy, "I've been buying used parts like those being sold in that parking lot at Stone Mountain, in those salvage yards back in Florida, at a tenth of what these guys are selling them for!" That was an epiphany for me! My entrepreneurial nature kicked in.

Back in Florida, I visited area salvage yards to scavenge for those used Mustang parts and factory accessories to resell.

Starting out, I scavenged anything early Mustang that I could find. Including scrubbing the used parts in our kitchen sink. My next-door neighbor felt sorry for me and stopped by my house one day with several old wheel covers he'd found along the roadside. I thanked him kindly and explained I only sold wheel covers for old Mustangs. He looked perplexed and didn't fully understand what I did for a living.

Scavenging salvage yards, aka junk yards; alarmingly, I learned that lots of varmints reside in old junk cars—spiders, snakes, lizards, and slimy frogs. Yuk! Thankfully, I was never bitten. Starting out, you'll have to experience many scary challenges on your road to success.

Early on, I would go to Ford dealers in the Southeast, asking the dealership's Parts Manager if they had any NOS (new old stock) Mustang parts or accessories they wanted to get rid of. Often, they did, since it had been more than a decade since the first Mustangs were introduced. At the time, few people were looking for early Mustang parts from 1965-1973 models. Parts Managers were glad to eliminate dated inventory, which burdened their parts budget. Those parts were a great find for me and my newly formed Mustang Supply Company.

I didn't start with a glossy magazine. I began with a newsletter format with only six legal-size printed pages, folded in half and stapled in the center, which created twelve pages. The original title was *The Mustang Exchange*

*Letter* for $7. Then, I changed the name to *Mustang Monthly Magazine* on the third issue.

Over time, my passion for Mustangs evolved into other American muscle cars of the '60s and '70s, prompting me to launch or purchase other magazines devoted to American performance cars. When I sold DPG, we were publishing a number of specialty automotive titles, including *Corvette Fever, Mopar Muscle, JP* (for Jeep, since Chrysler Corp would not allow us to use the Jeep name), *Super Ford, Muscle Car Review*, and others.

## Best Discoveries Typically Show Up When You're Doing Your Work

Early in my magazine's startup, Judy and I attended car shows and swap meets all over the Southeast. One event took place at Charlotte Motor Speedway in Charlotte, North Carolina, where a young man approached our booth and introduced himself.

He said, "My name is Donald Farr, and I see you've started a special interest magazine for Ford Mustangs."

He had an expensive camera hanging from his shoulder.

Then, he said, "I've been photographing several of the nice Mustangs at this event. If you'd like, I'll be glad to send the photos to you to feature in your magazine."

I told him it sounded great; however, I couldn't afford to pay him since the magazine wasn't profitable yet.

He said, "No worries, this is only my hobby and pastime. My regular job is working for my dad at his feed, seed, and fertilizer store in Union, South Carolina."

I gladly accepted his generous offer.

Within the following year, *Mustang Monthly Magazine* enjoyed excellent growth. Therefore, I called Donald and offered him the editor's position for *Mustang Monthly Magazine*. The starting salary was a pittance compared to today's standards. He told me he'd talk to his wife and let me know. Donald and his wife, Pam, had a baby at the time.

The next day, Donald called and told me they had rented a U-Haul Truck. He, his wife, and their baby daughter were moving to Florida to assume the editorial job. Nearly fifty years later, Donald is the Editor of *Mustang Times Magazine* and has written several automotive books.

I learned early on that sharecropping was demanding work with very little chance of a life of prosperity. Following in my daddy's footsteps to be a sharecropper was not for me. Thankfully, for Donald, following in his dad's footsteps to be a farm supplies and fertilizer store owner was not his goal in life.

## Starting Out, I Needed Skills I Didn't Have

After launching my magazine publishing business, I realized I didn't have the necessary publishing skills. Realistically, all I had was a desire to publish magazines devoted to the cars I loved. Therefore, I hired dedicated, competent people to work alongside me. They soon developed into the best! As my company grew, my philosophy was to hire good people with common sense and provide them with training. It worked.

Donald Farr was one of my first hires, and he certainly was the best. Today, Donald is known as an accomplished author, editor, and recognized authority on Ford Mustangs. His most recent full-color book, *Ford Mustang 60 Years*, is the latest example of his journalistic mastery.

## Train Competent Professionals and Retain Paid Advisors

*"People can't jump on your bandwagon if it's parked in your garage."*

—Sam Horn, The Intrigue Agency

When starting out, don't make the mistake of being a know-it-all. You'll go much farther being a learn-it-all. I discovered it's wise to find individuals with the various skills needed to accomplish tasks beyond your level of expertise.

I knew I needed people experienced in writing, editing, photography, art, layout and design, advertising sales, as well as information technology. Neither was I savvy enough to create and grow a magazine's circulation. Quite frankly, I had a lot to learn. Thus, I began looking for competent, qualified individuals with those skills. I also sought to hire people with these three essential character traits: integrity, passion, and savvy.

When your organization or business grows and becomes profitable, you'll want to consider developing your Workplace Leadership Team and, ultimately, obtain a Professional Advisory Group. These are knowledgeable professionals, not on your payroll. These professionals will provide objective input for your business or organization's future.

Also, this will prove beneficial if you decide to sell your company. Having a workplace leadership team and a professional advisory group in place will be valuable assets for the deal to go more smoothly and effectively. Quite frankly, unless you're planning to go solo in your business or career, you'll always need the help of others.

## Workplace Leadership Team

A few years after my publishing business had added enough subscribers and paid advertisers, I began building my Workplace Leadership Team. There were eight key people on this team. I was the President and CEO. Each department and each magazine had its own team comprised of five or six people, including many who worked remotely in other states. We had approximately seventy-five employees when I sold the company to an investment group that operated under the guise of Petersen Publishing. That company has been sold to foreign and United States buyers multiple times since then.

My policy for the Workplace Leadership Team was that it was comprised of individuals with integrity, passion, and the proven savvy needed for their individual leadership roles. This 8-person team was the heart of my publishing business. They stood beside me, holding up my hands when we passed through the rough waters of growth and economic cycles, which came occasionally.

## Professional Advisory Group

Then, when your business or organization grows even larger, you'll want to assemble a Professional Advisory Group comprised of professionals with expertise and skills to provide you with wise counsel. Choose only trusted professional advisors.

An Advisory Group typically consists of seasoned professionals. My in-house CFO and I were the only company employees in my Advisory Group. Note: This Group is not to be confused with a board of directors, i.e., stockholders. Instead, they're individuals with proven professional acumen who'll assist you with major operational decisions as paid professionals. They charge a fee for their counsel.

You should be willing to listen to and consider their ideas and opinions. However, don't allow your business or organization to be led by a committee as you're ultimately the one responsible for your success or failure. After you've heard their input, consider their opinions, pray, and make a leadership decision. Then, proactively act upon it.

## Hire Slow and Fire Fast

An example of hiring slowly happened when my staff accountant resigned to move out of state. I placed a 'want-ad' in the local newspaper. This was the pre-digital era. Soon, a young man answered the newspaper ad and applied for the leadership position. He had the educational credentials and the job skills qualifying him for the job, but his people skills, as reported by a previous employer, were not good. I told him I couldn't hire him. However, he was persistent and contacted me again. Again, I declined.

He was persistent. The third time he returned, I explained my reservations due to his previous employer's negative feedback, saying he had poor people skills.

With a forlorn look, he explained that no one had ever offered to invest in helping him improve his relationships and people skills. He said that if I were willing to invest in him, he would become one of the best people on my leadership team. I decided to give him a chance.

First, I had him attend Stephen Covey's "7 Habits of Highly Effective People" workshop and Dale Carnegie's "How to Win Friends & Influence People" seminars. We met twice a week to discuss his progress.

Within a few months, the people in his department told me how glad they were that I'd hired this young professional to be their department manager.

But, on a few occasions, I had to terminate an employee. Even when you do your best to hire only good people, there will be times when you must terminate someone whose personality or performance isn't the best for your business or organization. I learned the hard way that it is best to hire slow and fire fast.

## Delegate and Empower Your Team for Successful Leadership

My employees excelled because I empowered them to be the creative individuals they were created to be. People want to be trained, equipped, and empowered to accomplish their jobs while *singing or dancing* in their own creative way.

Workers who are trained and empowered only need to know what needs to be done. Let them decide how to get it done. I refer to this strategy as encouraging your eagles to SOAR. If you treat eagles like turkeys scratching in the dirt, they'll fly away.

## Your Eagles Must Be Allowed Opportunities to S.O.A.R.

I created this acronym when training my company's leadership team to excel.

**S**=SENSE OF PURPOSE "I must believe my work is making a difference."

**O**=OPPORTUNITY "I'll soar to new heights, given the opportunity to test my wings."

**A**= AUTHORITY "I must be provided with authority and adequate resources."

**R**=RECOGNITION "Share the recognition spotlight and the rewards with me."

Having a sense of purpose is the motivation needed for doing the work. You believe what you're doing matters.

You'll be more likely to feel fulfilled in your work when you're given opportunities to excel, showing your skills and competence.

Being authorized to make meaningful decisions and having the resources necessary to accomplish the desired results validates the job and one's feeling of worth.

Recognition is the most valuable tool in a leader's tool-kit. Share the recognition publicly and privately. Money is necessary, but recognition is an even more meaningful reward for a job done well.

Jesus taught his disciples to SOAR, equipping and empowering them to fulfill His Great Commission and to do so after He had departed.

*"If you employ people who are intelligent and who think for themselves, you must give them a lot of responsibility, as well as adequate resources and power, or they will leave you. Nobody wants to be a robot."*

–Charles Handy

When a company is well-managed, there will be signs, such as low employee turnover. Other markers of our success were two awards.

In 1994, the Florida Magazine Association awarded me the Publisher of the Year.

In 2008, I received the prestigious Lee Iacocca Award for "dedication to excellence in perpetuating an American automotive tradition." Lee Iacocca was the former president of Ford and Chrysler, two of the three giant American automotive companies. There are only

200 recipients of the Lee Iacocca Award. Other notable recipients include comedian and former host of "The Tonight Show" Jay Leno (a classic car enthusiast and collector), Carroll Shelby (a race car driver and designer), Bruce Meyer (a classic car collector), and Chip Foose (a custom car designer).

## A Wise Bargaining Tip

*"When negotiating, the first person who mentions money loses."*
—Larry G. Dobbs

The reason: When a value or asking price is mentioned, the other person knows exactly where the negotiating starts. If necessary, keep asking them the price. Let me explain. Whenever I purchased a competitor's magazine, I never mentioned how much I was willing to pay. On three separate occasions, I was prepared to pay hundreds of thousands more than the price the seller ultimately asked for.

On one occasion, I was prepared to pay $350,000 for another competitor's magazine. Yet, I never said I was willing to pay that amount. When the negotiations began, it turned out that the seller was in a financial bind and needed $50,000 quickly to get out of it. He told me that if I paid him cash before the coming weekend, he would take a total of $50,000 for his magazine. Thus, I saved $300,000 by not mentioning money first. Therefore, when negotiating a purchase, remember this powerful fact.

# REVIEW

- When starting out, you'll have to assume many roles. However, when your business gets big enough and becomes profitable, you'll want to be selective in choosing the leaders you'll invite on the journey with you.

- You might go faster if you go alone; however, you'll go further when you go together with the help of others. Get competent people to take the journey with you. I'm not talking about forming a partnership, of which I'm not a fan.

- Make wise decisions regarding the character and competence of those you are considering as team leaders. Make sure they're a complement to those who are already on your team. This makes the journey far more pleasant for everyone.

- When hiring team members, select good people with common sense. Then, provide the necessary training for their specific job description.

- When firing someone is necessary, do so fast, but be fair. When deserved, provide adequate severance pay, putting a check in their hand at dismissal time. And, if they're to be left on the payroll for a while, ensure you have a relationship contingency plan so they do not cause any ill will during that time.

- As your company or organization grows into a profitable, successful business, you will go farther with a trained Leadership Team. Also, use an Advisory Team of competent professionals to provide wise counsel as needed.

# 15
# ENCOURAGE OTHERS

*"Your opinion of me is a powerful mirror in my life… reflecting back, how I see myself."*

–Larry G. Dobbs

I WAS NOT the smartest kid in my fifth-grade class, but not the dumbest either. The truth is, I was very discouraged as an eleven-year-old. So, that's not why I remember the fifth grade. This is what I remember most about that year.

It was a cold January day when the lunch bell rang, and all my classmates hurried out toward the lunchroom. I remained at my desk, fidgeting with my notebook, pretending to be busy. That's when Mrs. Hampton, my fifth-grade teacher, walked to my desk and asked if I was going to the lunchroom. I didn't know how to answer her since I didn't have lunch money. This was long before government-funded lunch programs. So, I said, "No, ma'am, I'm not hungry today."

She said, "Well, Larry, I know today's your birthday. So, I'd like to buy your lunch."

I gladly accepted her offer because I was very hungry. Besides, it was Friday. On Fridays, we had a choice of fish or good hamburgers and chocolate milk. I remember it was a delicious lunch.

What I remembered most was Mrs. Hampton's words as we walked to the lunchroom.

She said, "Larry, I know you come from a large family of tenant farmers, and you have several brothers and sisters, which I'm sure makes things difficult. But, Larry, I also believe you're a smart young boy. And, if you work hard and apply yourself, God has a bright future for you. Just trust the Lord, son, do your best, and God will bless your life to become what He intends." Those words reminded me of my mother's similar words of encouragement.

In the second half of that year, I made all As, perhaps because of Mrs. Hampton's encouraging words that day. I did great until I became a know-it-all in the ninth grade.

This true story is an example of the power of what we say to someone who needs encouragement or affirmation. Remember, your words have the power of life and death. Statistics show that destructive words to someone who's feeling down can be all it takes to kill them. Sharing words of encouragement can shed light and hope in their life.

We are likely to give up when we believe we can't change the outcome in a difficult situation. Conversely, when we receive encouragement from someone who believes that we can do better, we will usually do better.

As a LifeSkills teacher, I created an 'Encouragement' folder. It contains encouraging letters, emails, and notes from individuals I have had the opportunity to know, lead, teach, and interact with. Occasionally, I open it up to remind myself how blessed and grateful I am to have had the opportunity to invest in the lives of these individuals. On days when I need a pick-me-up, I will take out the folder to remind myself, "Don't give up, Larry, you can make it today!"

Encouragement is not flattery or empty praise. It's like verbal sunshine. It costs nothing, but it warms our hearts, inspiring hope and confidence. I always used the 80:20 rule when an employee needed correcting. I tried to incorporate at least 80% of the discussion toward their positive traits and value to the company, and no more than 20% about areas needing improvement.

*"A candle loses nothing when it lights another candle."*

–Thomas Jefferson

# REVIEW

- The gift of encouragement is not expensive but highly valuable.
- People need encouragement most when they deserve it least.
- Encouragement is an investment that pays exponential dividends.
- To make a difference in another's life, become an encourager.
- An encourager is a conduit of God's grace, mercy, and hope.
- Don't confuse encouragement with enabling. Always be kind but truthful.
- Encouragers help you facilitate your dreams, while discouragers seek to frustrate your dreams. Thus, be careful about who you associate with.
- An encourager is a creative thinker; discouragers are destructive thinkers.
- Encouragers help you have the faith to focus on God and His promises; discouragers remind you of the odds you face.

*"Treat a man as he is, and he'll remain as he is. Treat a man as he can and should be, and he'll become the man he can and should be."*

—JOHANN WOLFGANG VON GOETHE

# PART 2

# NUGGETS OF WISDOM

### 1. How to make wise decisions in controversial situations.

Wisdom's first step is to become knowledgeable. Couple that knowledge with a deeper understanding to make sound judgments and informed decisions. You can only do so by being a patient and attentive listener, seeking to gain a better overall understanding, especially in controversial situations. You're wise to view conflicting opinions as an opportunity to become better informed. Be inquisitive. Ask open-ended questions. Accept others' feelings as valid, even though their facts might be flawed, so they'll feel understood, and you'll be more capable of making a wise decision in the situation.

> *"Wisdom is enshrined in an understanding heart; wisdom is not found among fools."*
> (Proverbs 14:33 New Living Translation)

### 2. Making wise decisions and exhibiting competence will create a lasting legacy.

Your reputation shows what others think of you as a person; while your legacy is the difference you make in the lives of others, your family, the community, and in the world. To become spiritually mature, commit to growing in the grace and knowledge of God. The quality of your personal relationships is the best indicator of the legacy you are creating. Spiritual maturity is evidenced by being caring, kind, and generous. These are exemplary character traits of someone with a positive, lasting legacy. The world will know.

> *"But as for me and my family, we will serve the Lord."* (Joshua 24:15 New Living Translation)

## 3. Choose to be other-centered.

When selfishness walks in, caring and compassion walk out. Being other-centered means you're more concerned about relationships than about yourself. This requires God's anointing to show empathy and kindness. God's Holy Spirit will help you become considerate in your words and actions. Seek a 'win-win' when making decisions. The notable differences between being self-led and being Spirit-led are illustrated in Scripture as acts of the flesh (Galatians 5:19-21) compared to the fruit of the Spirit (Galatians 5:22-23).

> *"Instead of asking yourself, How am I doing today?, ask, How are those I care about doing today?"* –Larry G. Dobbs

## 4. Don't quit.

We all experience failures and disappointments. Failures and disappointments are often beyond our control. This is the time for being resilient. Seek God's wisdom, prayerfully believing that positive things will happen when we don't give up. Practice doesn't make perfect, only consistent. Therefore, continually evaluate and make improvements to identify the necessary changes for success.

> *"Success is never final; failure is never fatal.*
> *It's the courage to continue that counts."* —
> UCLA Basketball Coach John Wooden

## 5. When correcting someone, end the conversation with encouragement.

Perhaps, most importantly, these conversations should be private. As a parent, teacher, or mentor, there are times you'll have to provide correction and guidance. Apply the 20:80 rule, spend twenty percent of the conversation about the problem and the correction needed, then spend eighty percent about the person's strengths and accomplishments. By doing so, the person can leave the meeting with an understanding of their mistake, as well as having hope for the future.

> *"So, encourage each other and build each*
> *other up, just as you are already doing."* (1
> Thessalonians 5:11 New Living Translation)

## 6. Joy is a Christian's Certificate of Authenticity.

You can't always control what happens in your life. God's Holy Spirit can enable you, as a believer, to maintain an attitude of joy. You do so by believing that He is always there, always with you. Culture will suggest you throw in the towel and buckle under. Yet, because of God's promise of your salvation and eternal life, you can always trust in His powerful promises, empowered to remain joyous, even when life brings those times of grief and disappointment.

*"Dear brothers and sisters, when troubles of any kind come your way, consider it an opportunity for great joy. For you know that when your faith is tested, your endurance has a chance to grow. So let it grow, for when your endurance is fully developed, you will be perfect and complete, needing nothing."* (James 1:2-4 New Living Translation)

## 7. The unexpected does not take God by surprise.

When the unexpected happens in your life, pray instead of fretting and worrying. Ask the Holy Spirit to shift your focus from your problem to His Holy presence. He alone has the power and anointing to offer you the peace that is beyond your finite mind's understanding. Therefore, prayer should be the first thing you do when life becomes too difficult and overwhelming. God's awaiting your call.

*"Be still in the presence of the Lord, and wait patiently for Him to act."* (Psalms 37:7 New Living Translation)

## 8. Be enthusiastic!

Enthusiasm is the outward evidence of your inner confidence. Enthusiasm is the result of how you think. A positive attitude is shown in your conversations and daily behavior. When you are enthusiastic about something, it stimulates your passion and creativity. Enthusiasm is virtually impossible to conceal as you go about your activities. You're apt to be asked, "What is on your mind that's gotten you so upbeat?" If you could bottle it up and sell it, the world would beat a path to your door. Remember when you first became a believer? You were excited, knowing that God had transformed your life now…and for all eternity.

> *"Don't copy the behavior and customs of this world, but let God transform you into a new person by changing the way you think. Then you will learn to know God's will for you, which is good and pleasing and perfect."* (Romans 12:2 New Living Translation)

## 9. Lift others up.

Almost everyone desires to be admired, respected, and complimented. Yet, most don't receive the recognition and respect they long for. Focus the conversation on the other person and his accomplishments. Express sincere interest in what he says and what's going on in his life. When you do so, he will appreciate it and think well of you. When you seek to bring out the best in others, they'll be encouraged.

> *"Don't be selfish; don't try to impress others. Be humble, thinking of others as better than yourselves. Don't look out only for your own interest, but take an interest in others, too. You must have the same attitude as Christ Jesus had."* (Philippians 2:3-5 New Living Translation)

## 10. Identify your unique giftings to be inspired to pursue God's calling in life.

What is it that causes you to feel energized and excited when you're doing it? For example, people say that you're very good at this. God has gifted you with the skills for accomplishing this work or activity. You have a feeling of fulfillment when performing this task. This is definitely in your skill wheelhouse.

> *"Don't ask yourself what the world needs. Ask yourself what makes you come alive, and go do that. Because what the world needs are people who have come alive."* —Gil Bailie, Founder and President of Cornerstone Forum

## 11. Beware of dream vampires.

The most important thing in achieving your dream is to have one! The great inventions and advancements in history were ridiculed by dream vampires. The world is filled with discouragers. Your dreams open doors to a new future, giving you the courage to achieve and become. Dreams are seldom shared by others, not even family and friends. Don't expect the town to cheer you on or see you off when you board the bus, going toward your dreams. Remember, you've got to believe it if you ever hope to see it.

> *"If you've got a dream, chase it, cause a dream won't chase you back."* —Lyrics from Cody Johnson's song "'Til You Can't"

## 12. Pride is the enemy's trap.

Focus instead on building others up; doing so will improve how you feel about yourself. Also, it is foolish to spend all your time focusing on tasks (work, ministry, and/or career) because your relationships will suffer. No one lying on their deathbed has ever said, "My biggest regret was not spending more time at work." True success is in the journey, not the destination. If you're not enjoying the journey, chances are, you won't like the destination either. Don't climb to the top of the ladder of success, only to discover it was leaning against the wrong wall. Therefore, remember, your relationships have greater value than work or accomplishments.

*"Through pride, we are ever deceiving ourselves. Since deep down below the surface of our conscience, a still, small voice says to us, Something is out of tune."* —Chris Jami

## 13. You can have a valuable influence on the lives of others.

You can influence me by what you're saying, but only momentarily. You influence me by what you know, but that, too, is temporary. It's what you do for me, and how you make me feel, that will create a lasting influence in my life. It's important to remember that to the world, you may be only one person. But to one, you may be the world. Become that positive difference in someone's life today. Never underestimate the power of your influence. Kind words of encouragement are valuable investments in the lives of those whom you influence.

Here's what my daddy told me about influence, before passing away:

*"I don't have any money to leave you, son, but remember this: the only inheritance a man can leave that will last for all eternity is his influence."* —Charlie V. Dobbs Sr.

## 14. Offering understanding, even though you might not agree, shows that you care.

When someone shares their feelings, the main thing they're looking for is understanding. Therefore, remember, while their facts might be flawed, their feelings are valid. Even if you disagree with their facts, try to be understanding. There are three things we look for in a friend: someone who'll listen, offer understanding, and validate our feelings. It's okay to ask questions about what they're sharing. Since discussing the situation will give each of you a better insight, it also shows that you're interested. Never attack anyone's feelings.

*"Understand this, my dear brothers and sisters: You must be quick to listen, slow to speak, and slow to get angry. Human anger does not produce the righteousness God desires."* (James 1:19-20 New Living Translation)

## 15. Are you living every day as if it is Groundhog Day?

Then, this year will be no different from last year. Don't blame procrastination for the inability to make the right decision. Procrastination is a tragic decision to put off living. Thus, you'll spend your life caught between a rock and a hard place of indecision.

> *"Farmers who wait for perfect weather never plant.*
> *If they watch every cloud, they never harvest."*
> (Ecclesiastes 11:4 New Living Translation)

## 16. Become a lifelong learner; it's the pathway to wisdom and longevity.

Statistics show that lifelong learners typically live happier and longer lives.

Caution: The second half of life can be deadly, mostly because of one's mindset. The natural progression of human nature in the second half of life is to transition from being productive to being comfortable, then to complacency. Complacency leads to firmness of mind. Finally, your brain becomes like cement, and your mind is set, impossible to stir. Stay relevant, reinvent yourself, and thrive!

> *"The illiterate of the 21ˢᵗ century will not be those who*
> *cannot read or write, but those unwilling to learn, unlearn,*
> *and relearn."* —Alvin Toffler, Author of *Future Shock*

## 17. The person who is humble and brave enough to ask questions is wise.

Good news for those of us who don't have a high IQ. Research shows we're more apt to be open-minded, willing to ask questions, and try new things. Children explore what they don't know, constantly asking questions. While adults tend to exploit what they already know. Great leaders aren't so much smarter than everyone else; rather, it's their willingness to ask questions, seeking to learn more about what they don't already know. Thus, becoming wiser.

> *"Cry out for insight, and ask for understanding. Search for them as you would for silver; seek them like hidden treasures."* (Proverbs 2:3-4 New Living Translation)

## 18. Positivity energizes. Negativity drains.

Positive thoughts and positive conversations keep you energized. While negative thoughts and negative conversations are energy suckers. Your attitude, for better or worse, impacts your relationships more than anything, including appearance, intellect, or skills. Companies and organizations typically hire people for their expertise and job skills. Yet, statistics have proven that the best hires are those who are hired for the right attitude and then trained in the required skills. Statistics reveal that people with a positive attitude are more likely to excel in performance and teamwork, proving to be the most valuable team members.

> *"Attitude is a little thing that makes a big difference."* —Winston Churchill

## 19. As the team leader, do what you do best and delegate the rest.

The more skilled and competent your team members become, the less you'll have to oversee them. First, find, select, and hire only those who want to be on the journey with you and can complete the journey. I recommend hiring people based on their attitude, then training them for the skills they need for the task. Be patient. Remember, empowerment is not a quick process.

> *"In his grace, God has given us different gifts for doing certain things well."* (Romans 12:6 New Living Translation)

## 20. Mutual awareness creates mutual understanding.

A shared awareness among family members ensures a shared understanding. Mutual awareness, more than anything, will avoid unmet expectations. If you want others to buy in, you must keep them in the know of what's going on. However, when you share goals or plans, be prepared to answer their questions. The better everyone understands, the better the chances of successful results. The more open and trusting your relationships are, the deeper the understanding. Sharing information shows they're valued and builds trust.

*"When you treat people like flowers, they blossom, but when you treat them like weeds, they shrivel."* —Charles Handy

## 21. Older doesn't mean wiser; practice doesn't make perfect, only consistent.

The older you get and the more you learn, the more you know you don't know. We are inundated with technological advancements, savvy artificial intelligence, and scientific discoveries. Yet, few are becoming wiser. What's missing is a lack of Spiritual wisdom. Godly wisdom and understanding can only be achieved from studying Scriptures, praying, and listening attentively to God's Holy Spirit, making a habit of seeking His wisdom daily.

> *"Fear of the Lord is the foundation of true knowledge, but fools despise wisdom and discipline."*
> (Proverbs 1:7 New Living Translation)

## 22. Persistence is not discovered on the starting line, but in your response to the challenges you'll encounter while running the race.

Everyone can look sharp before the race begins, but the one who has the determination to stay in the race with an unwavering expectation of victory will be the one who'll be standing proudly in the winner's circle when the race ends.

> *"Blessed is the one who perseveres under trial because, having stood the test, that person will receive the crown of life that the Lord has promised to those who love him."* (James 1:12 New Living Translation)

## 23. When things seem out of control, competent leaders exercise self-control.

Leadership means having the courage to stand up and demonstrate that you are aware of the situation and have the competence to restore order. Often, when my company was facing dire financial conditions, I would call a company-wide meeting to show everyone that things would be all right. I'd explain the steps we'd take to get finances back in line. Then, everyone was willing to pitch in and do their part to help. Remember, courage is essential for the leader.

> *"The calmer you are under pressure, the more likely you'll succeed as a leader. As calmness of mind is one of the beautiful jewels of wisdom."* —James Allen

## 24. Becoming a person of influence requires investing in the lives of others.

As a parent, team leader, or mentor, those you influence look to you as a source of knowledge and motivation to accomplish their potential. Be willing to invest the time and energy to help them achieve their goals. Your influence on their life will be directly related to the overall investment you've made.

In Galatians 5:22-23, Saint Paul shares nine essential attributes of a sought-after influencer: Love, Joy, Peace, Patience, Kindness, Goodness, Faithfulness, Gentleness, and Self-control.

## 25. Identify workers' strengths and what they do best, not what you do best.

In my magazine publishing company, each magazine typically had 3-5 people on its team; Donald Farr, the editorial director of all the magazines, had both writing and photography expertise, as well as knowing the job an individual was best suited for. Dobbs Publishing Group was blessed to have a leader with his understanding of all facets of creating a successful magazine. He was an inspirational leader, always trying to inspire his teams, never resorting to command and control. Thus, he was an expert at leading teams. If you're seeking to hire or train the right person for the right job, first evaluate what they're best at. Then, encourage them to improve their strengths and not waste time and energy trying to improve their weaknesses.

*"When a leader resorts to command and control, inspiration leaves the building." —Leading in Crisis* by Bill George

## 26. Embrace who you are.

Whom do you want to be like? Be you, everyone else is taken. You were not created to be someone else. Decide to begin today and become the best version of who you are meant to be. Tell the person in the mirror that today will be a new beginning for you and for your life. Resist anyone who tries to tell you that you can't be exactly who you are.

*"To be yourself in a world that is constantly*

*trying to make you something else is your greatest
accomplishment."* —Ralph Waldo Emerson

## 27. The man who thinks he's too big to respect others is just too big for his britches.

Often, the haughty person who exhibits a disrespectful attitude is trying to hide an inferiority complex. Being prideful and braggadocios turns people off more than anything. Trying to mask anxiety and stress can cause individuals to resort to being disrespectful, which is typical of someone struggling with low self-esteem. Remember, Jesus washed the feet of his disciples.

*"If you think you are too important to help someone, you are only fooling yourself. You are not that important."*
(Galatians 6:3 New Living Translation)

## 28. No vision? No need for a leader. Why? A leader's vision creates the foundation, the roadmap the team will need for their journey.

When drafting your organization's vision statement, solicit input from all those who'll take the journey with you. Remember, some of the best ideas come from the people on the front line. Talk with them and listen. Sharing your vision will quickly separate those who want to help you create the future from those who only want to re-create the past. Follow these criteria for selecting the right participants:

- People who have the necessary skills.

- People who want to go where you'll take them, and most of all,
- People who want to be on the bus with those people taking the trip.

*"In the future, the great leaders will be those who figure out how to tap into their people's hearts… their passions, and desires to make a difference in their work."*—Bill George, former CEO of Medtronic, Author of *Authentic Leadership*

## 29. If you give to God by the teaspoon, don't expect Him to bless you by the truckload.

There are many ways you can give to God. Scripture tells us that 10% of our income belongs to God, as a tithe. When questioning whether the title is based on gross income or net income, simply decide if you want God's gross blessings or His net blessings. Amounts given for special offerings, such as missions and benevolence, are in addition to the tithe. Malachi 3:10 is the only place that God explicitly encourages people to test Him regarding their willingness to tithe. Jesus also reiterates the results of being a faithful supporter of God's Kingdom:

*"… and with the measure you use, it will be measured to you."* (Matthew 7:2 New International Version)

## 30. Appreciate what you have.

Striving to acquire more stuff? Instead, choose to be content with what you have. Because the more stuff you have, the more hassle you'll have. Caring relationships are what provide hope and happiness, not stuff. Nurture your meaningful relationships, and you'll be more fulfilled and happier in life. Make a daily habit of connecting with the people who are important to you. Remember that which you nurture will thrive, and that which you neglect will die. Consider keeping a daily Gratitude Journal. According to Psychologist Sonja Lyubomirsky, "One of the proven ways to move the happiness needle is by keeping a Gratitude Journal." Lyubomirsky's research found that engaging in meaningful activities, such as serving others, can create feelings of contentment.

> *"Gratitude is the fairest blossom that springs*
> *from the soul."* —Henry Ward Beecher

## 31. No one cares what you know until they know that you care.

The influential person is more concerned with how they make listeners feel about themselves, such as what's important to them. You can easily make a point in conversation, but that's not nearly as important as making a difference. A key requirement for becoming an influential leader is selflessness. That's why so few leaders are truly influential. You must be willing to invest in people's lives, make sacrifices, and help them change to become better. When you do so, you'll be a positive influence in their lives.

> *"If you're able to inspire others to dream more,*
> *learn more, do more, and become more, you are an*
> *influential leader."* —John Quincy Adams

## 32. Do your good thoughts about friends and loved ones turn into actions?

People are lonely, dying on the inside, desperately in need of someone who is willing to offer themselves and their time. Our relationships struggle when they lack good deeds. Ask God to anoint you to be a friend to someone that He's laid on your heart, with a word of encouragement. If it's an elderly person, ask if you can run an errand, take them to an appointment, or to the grocery store. At the end of the day, people won't always remember what you said or did, but they will remember how you made them feel.

> *"You cannot do a kindness too soon, for you never know when it will be too late."* —Ralph Waldo Emerson

## 33. Are you hoping someone will change and improve? Your best strategy is to change and improve the person looking back at you in the mirror.

When self-reflection is viewed objectively, you've begun the process of becoming more aware of what you need to change. I discovered the hard way; you can't change people. You'll have more success evaluating areas in your life that need change. Interestingly, when we focus on improving personal traits, we're apt to witness those around us appear to be changing for the better. Changing your motives refocuses the change you desire from external to internal. Begin slowly, list three areas you'd like to improve. If you're a Christian, ask the Holy Spirit to help you see those areas. And, if you have a close friend whom you truly trust, ask them to also help you identify what you need to change and improve.

> *"There is only one corner of the universe you can be certain of improving, and that's your own self."*

## 34. Activity doesn't mean you're making progress.

To make meaningful progress, you must first establish your ultimate goal. From there, create step-by-step goals to assess your progress. With these incremental goals, you'll be able to see where you are, as well as measure your progress. Therefore, you'll be able to focus on effectiveness instead of getting sidetracked on rabbit trails or busyness. You'll discover that real progress is accomplished by prioritizing the quality of actions over quantity.

> *"Do not confuse motion with progress. Put your money in that little electric pony at Wal-Mart, ride it fast as you can, when it stops, you're still at Wal-Mart."* –Larry G. Dobbs

## 35. Encourage and train others to be teachers in the organization.

Strong interpersonal relationships are great for both the teacher and student when they have a better understanding of the business or organization, i.e., a sense of buy-in and ownership. At my company, I encouraged my leaders to spend time with their team, training and equipping them for their assigned roles. Additionally, this created a rapport between the leader and the employee whom they'd trained.

> *"When your people are emotionally invested, they're more apt to contribute."* –Larry G. Dobbs

## 36. Do you have ten years' experience, or just one year's experience repeated ten times over?

What different roles or jobs have you had during the past ten years? What career achievements have you had? List career advancement books, seminars, and workshops you've attended in those ten years. List continuing educational curriculum completed.

Therefore, is your experience that you've been doing the same thing for the past ten years?

> *"Develop a passion for learning. If you do, you will never cease to grow."* —Anthony J. D'Angelo

## 37. Without self-improvement, you'll never experience self-advancement.

Personal growth and advancement go hand-in-hand. Self-confidence is the key benefit of always seeking to improve yourself, in every way, personal, professional, and spiritual. Now is the best time to discover your strengths. Then, begin improving them, as they are God's gift to you, individually, as His unique creation. You'll accomplish all He desires when you continually develop and improve yourself.

*"Do the best you can until you know better. Then, when you know better, do better."* —Maya Angelou

## 38. Don't allow your dreams and decisions to be based upon the rules and opinions written out of the fears and failures of others.

Start out with what you know. You may dream of building a sports car. But if all you have are the parts of a soapbox, begin building a soapbox. The 700 hp sports car with Michelin tires on its fancy 20-inch wheels can be added one part at a time. To achieve something exponential, you've got to be willing to begin with the incremental, like a soapbox.

*"Naysayers are the loudest voices you hear when starting out. Nevertheless, continue on."* –Larry G. Dobbs

## 39. Having a positive attitude about a project, without planning, hard work, and perseverance, will result in nothing more than grandiose expectations.

A positive attitude is fine, it provides fuel. However, expect challenges and contradictions as you progress. Prepare to embrace boundaries and reality. Planning will provide the roadmap you'll need for the project's completion. Additionally, a well-researched and thought-out plan will assist in obtaining outside financing. Do it first! A positive attitude with passion is more fun but less reliable than good planning.

> *"My child, don't lose sight of common sense and*
> *discernment. Hang on to them, for they will refresh*
> *your soul. They are like jewels on a necklace. They keep*
> *you safe on your way, and your feet will not stumble."*
> (Proverbs 3:21-23 New International Version)

## 40. Perhaps it's time to create balance in your life by creating a 'To-Don't' list.

Authentic individuals lead balanced lives personally, professionally, and spiritually. Recently, my pastor gave an altar invitation to those who needed prayer and were struggling with stress. Over one hundred responded. My good friend, Reverend Jim Campbell, says the way he evaluates whether to agree to do a thing someone asks is by knowing it's okay to say, "No," if there's a deeper "Yes" in his life's schedule. If you're married, after God, but before everyone and everything else, including work and ministry, make your spouse your top priority. No amount of success at work will compensate for failure at home.

> *"Don't give the best of yourself to the people who*
> *care about you the least at the expense of those*
> *who care about you the most."* —Author and
> Men's Ministry leader, Patrick Morley

## 41. People are more likely to embrace change when they are kept fully informed.

At Dobbs Publishing Group, I tried to keep employees informed about changes that would affect them. The company's individual leaders would also explicitly share, in detail, what was going to change and how it would affect their department. This helped by giving everyone an opportunity to be a part of the process. Unless people are kept informed and know what to expect, they'll succumb to retreating into what they know, their comfort zones. All because leadership was afraid to do what they should have done.

> *"What you were trained to do, what you did yesterday, were gifts from your past. Begin by saying, 'what I used to do was …' This is a great way to open the door to … ' what I'm going to be doing tomorrow.'"*
> —Seth Godin, Author and Marketing Expert

## 42. When you get on the bus, pursuing your dreams, likely no one will be there to see you off. However, when you return as a hero, everyone will be there to greet you.

In the movie, *The Rookie*, Dennis Quaid starred as Jim Morris, the man who was a rookie baseball pitcher. The true story begins when Morris was a high school coach at Reagan County High School in Big Lake, Texas, a small town of 3,000 people. He had always wanted to be a professional baseball pitcher, but he never pursued his dream, instead settling for coaching a small-town high school team. His high school players witnessed how hard and accurate he could pitch, so they challenged him to try out for the pros. Morris, in turn, told them if they'd win their first-ever state championship, he'd try out for the major leagues. They won the championship! Then, in his mid-thirties, everyone thought Morris was crazy when he got on the bus that night to pursue his dream. Morris tried out and was sent to the minor leagues before finally being called up to the majors. Ultimately, he made his Major League debut for the Tampa Bay Rays on September 18, 1999, pitching against the Texas Rangers in Arlington, Texas, at the age of thirty-five. He struck out Royce Clayton with four pitches. Virtually everybody from Big Lake, Texas, was there, cheering him on. Another famous star said this to Elvis Presley when he performed that first night at The Grand Ole Opry:

> *"Son, you oughta go back to driving a truck. You sure ain't ever gonna be an entertainer."*

## 43. When deciding whether to invest in a romantic relationship, ask, Is there electricity? If there's no spark, don't buy lightbulbs.

When there's no spark, it won't be long until the romantic lights go out. Romantic love struggles to survive without the spark that attracts, kindling the flames, the emotional requisites of a romantic relationship. However, once your relationship becomes a loving one, loving feelings must be accompanied by loving actions. True love is a lifetime commitment to otherness, an unconditional decision to serve the needs, growth, and fulfillment of another, having an ongoing willingness to nurture the relationship with loving actions. God intended that true love be a love that lasts forever.

*"Three things will last forever—faith, hope,
and love—and the greatest of these is love." (1
Corinthians 13:13 New Living Translation)*

## 44. When you talk the talk, some will listen. When you walk the walk, people will follow.

I've learned a lot just by listening to and watching other people. Some were wise, most were not. I learned that, in the end, not enough that mattered was being done. That's when I asked God to give me the wisdom to begin teaching and training people to improve their LifeSkills. Over the past three decades, hundreds have attended my classes and workshops. These wisdom nuggets are a partial compilation of those teachings.

*"As influencers, we have all been given such a
precious gift. With that gift comes an awesome
responsibility to make a difference in the world."*
—Barbara Glanz, National Speakers Association

## 45. When I'm brave enough to leave certainty behind, I can rise above the wall that separates your views from mine.

Too often, we allow our preconceived opinions and beliefs to close our minds to any other view. The fact is, we've got our minds made up and don't want to be confused by the facts. There's a huge difference between being open-minded and empty-headed. You can convince the latter of most anything, true, false, or fantasy, they'll believe it.

But the ability to listen, with the intent to understand an opposing viewpoint, is a sign of true wisdom. This will not only open the door to getting the other person to accept your point of view, but you'll also have a much better chance of convincing them that your viewpoint is correct.

> *"If there is any secret of success, it lies in the ability to get the other person's point of view and see things from his angle as well as from your own."* —Henry Ford

## 46. Choose risk takers to begin. As your business or organization grows, add caretakers.

When starting out, it's wise to seek counsel from professionals who have the expertise to advise you. However, you'll also want team members running alongside you who have the passion to help you excel quickly. Initially, when I launched my publishing company, it was just my wife and me. Then, I hired a young artist with sales skills to help put the magazine together and sell advertising. Next, there came internal support workers. After about a year, I hired my first editor/photographer. We were off and running. Thereafter, I hired a bookkeeper/accountant. Initially, you'll have to wear many hats. Just progress at a reasonable pace and you'll be fine.

> *"A crackpot is a man who's chasing a new idea—until he succeeds."* —Mark Twain

## 47. Regardless of how independent you think you are, you'll need others' help to succeed.

Your spouse can be someone who can walk alongside you. Then, as your endeavor grows, look for others who have skills and strengths to compensate for your weaknesses, as well as those to complement your skills. I personally experienced the wise counsel offered by King Solomon regarding the added strength of having helpers taking the journey. See Ecclesiastes 4:9-10. "Two people are better off than one, for they can help each other succeed. If one person falls, the other can reach out and help. But someone who falls alone is in real trouble."

*"Great things in business and organizations are never done by one person. They're always done by a team of people."* —Steve Jobs, founder of Apple

## 48. What if you cry out to God and don't get an answer?

I have been there. It was 1998. I sold my successful magazine publishing company for over thirty times its earnings. My wife and I were excited about what the future might hold. I was fifty-four years old, planning to expand my leadership training and LifeSkills teaching, and traveling. Then, my wife called from the doctor's office to say they'd discovered that she had a brain tumor. We'd been happily married for twenty-five years and were devastated. For the next seven years, we, along with our family and thousands of others, prayed diligently. We were referred to cancer specialists in several states. She underwent heartbreaking tests and procedures. We never quit praying. Yet, God didn't answer. We lost the battle, and my darling wife passed away peacefully in March of 2005. Nevertheless, I didn't turn my back on Him or my salvation. I didn't understand why it wasn't God's will to heal her. Losing Judy was the toughest thing I've ever suffered. Thankfully, I look forward to seeing her in heaven. How strong is your faith?

> *"My Father! If it is possible, let this cup of suffering be taken away from me. Yet, I want your will to be done, not mine."* (Matthew 26:39 New Living Translation)

## 49. It's impossible to manage your time if you give it all away.

Perhaps the greatest benefit of being a better manager of your time is that you'll be more productive and less stressed. I've got a saying about having too many irons in the fire: "I'm expressed!" Which, translated, means I'm excited and stressed. When you effectively manage your time, you'll discover you're more organized and efficient. Twenty years ago, the buzz was to multitask. Today, the time management gurus recommend focusing on and completing one task at a time. As a bonus, you'll be more decisive as you evaluate daily activities. That's what works best for me.

> *"Until you can manage your time, you can manage nothing else."* —Peter Drucker

## 50. This is the day that the Lord has made. Rejoice and be glad in it.

The best way to start your day is to get up and make your bed. Schedule activities that matter, such as Bible study and time alone with God. Choose healthy eating habits, nurture meaningful relationships, review long-term goals, engage in regular physical activity, and maintain your personal health. Navy Admiral William H. McRaven, a four-star Admiral and retired Navy SEAL, applied the daily habit of making his bed before anything else every morning. His commencement speech at the University of Texas was based upon his lifestyle and the positive results and importance of starting your day right, if you hoped to have a good day, a day of rejoicing and gladness. Small actions, such as starting your day with a small accomplishment, can make all the difference in having a good day.

> *"The secret of your success is determined by your daily agenda."* —John C. Maxwell

# AFTERWORD: REINVENT YOUR LIFE

After selling Dobbs Publishing Group, I became inspired to reinvent my life for a new purpose. My newly acquired passion was now researching, teaching relationship and leadership skills, and mentoring people to pursue God's calling for their lives.

One of the programs I created was a weekly LifeSkills class. It provided daily practical knowledge for developing the people skills, relationship skills, leadership skills, and other skills necessary for success in life and a career.

The class quickly grew in attendance to over 150 people. Due to the class size, I selected an eight-person leadership team to assist with class functions, allowing me to focus on studying, researching, and creating the curriculum I presented each week.

Soon, my church's pastor asked me to become our church's Leadership Training Director (pro bono). That's when I launched a one-year leadership training program for emerging leaders entitled "The Joshua Group." Many of those "Joshua Group" graduates lead various businesses, churches, and communities today.

A powerful fact I've learned as a leader is that each success happened with the help and assistance of competent, dedicated people working alongside me. In conclusion, if you only want to go *fast* in life, go alone. But if you want to go *far*, you'll need to go together, with the help of others.

Perhaps you're at a point in life when God is directing you to reinvent yourself and to begin investing in the success of others. If so, you'll discover it's very rewarding to have those you've influenced express their appreciation for your positive influence in their lives.

# ACKNOWLEDGMENTS

There have been so many extraordinary individuals who've played a part in my accomplishments. Here are a few of them:

- Charlie V. Dobbs Sr. and Sarah Elizabeth Parks Dobbs, my devoted, loving, and hard-working parents.
- Charlie V. Dobbs Jr., my oldest brother, mentored me as a young man, allowing me to discover a love for cars and trucks.
- Mrs. Hampton, the encouraging, sweet lady who was my fifth-grade teacher at Culbertson Elementary School.
- Judy Ann Summerlin Dobbs (1952-2005), my beautiful, loving wife of thirty years and mother of our two sons.
- My two devoted sons, Jason Eric Dobbs and Joshua Lee Dobbs, of whom I'm very proud and love with all my heart.
- My grandson, Landon, who is becoming a mature Christian young man.
- Melody Hume Dobbs, my loving wife, who brought love, joy, and purpose back to my life.
- My newest son, Nathan Poole (Melody's son), who

graciously offered input on the content of this book.

- Jenna Poole, Nathan's beautiful wife and mother of our four granddaughters, Faith, Brianna, Hannah, and Natallie. All sweet little angels.
- My pastor and best friend for nearly forty years, Reverend M. Wayne Blackburn, and his beautiful wife, Sharon. The Blackburns are wonderful friends.
- My loving extended family, who are always so kind and caring.
- My close friends of over forty years, Dennis Harrison and Mark Steinmetz, and my good friend, Gary Ballard, are in my small group at Victory Church.
- From my business life, the following significantly contributed to my success: The Dobbs Publishing Group Leadership Team, including Donald Farr, Kathy Willis, Kevin Miller, Mike Wells, Howard Buck, and Curt Patterson.
- Additionally, all my talented coworkers and employees were integral to Dobbs Publishing Group's success.
- The following individuals provided wise counsel in selling my publishing company: Chas Smith, Ron Clark, Clay Hall, René Gnam, and Les Sufrin.

> *"Yet I am confident I will see the Lord's goodness*
> *while I'm here in the land of the living."*
> (Psalm 27:13 New Living Translation)

# ABOUT THE AUTHOR

Larry G. Dobbs is a distinguished figure in the world of automotive publishing and leadership, best known for his role as President and CEO of Dobbs Publishing Group in Lakeland, Florida. Over a career spanning more than two decades, he built a legacy as an innovative publisher and marketing consultant, shaping the landscape of specialty automotive magazines.

Dobbs received the prestigious **Lee Iacocca Award** for "dedication to excellence in perpetuating an American automotive tradition." Jay Leno is a fellow recipient of the award. Mr. Dobbs was also named **Publisher of the Year** by the Florida Magazine Association for publishing excellent automobile magazines, including *Mustang Monthly*, *Corvette Fever*, and other car magazines.

Beyond his publishing achievements, Dobbs is recognized for his commitment to mentoring emerging leaders and his contributions to the Lakeland business community. His career embodies entrepreneurial leadership rooted in passion, adaptability, and a deep respect for both his audience and his team.

www.ingramcontent.com/pod-product-compliance
Lightning Source LLC
Chambersburg PA
CBHW061759120626
46550CB00005B/2054